Vincentia Schroeter, Margit Koemeda-Lutz, Ma[...]
Bioenergetic Analysis 2008 (1[...]

»edition psychosozial«

Vincentia Schroeter, Margit Koemeda-Lutz,
Maê Nascimento (Eds.)

Bioenergetic Analysis

The Clinical Journal of the International Institute for
Bioenergetic Analysis (2008) Volume 18

Psychosozial-Verlag

Bibliografische Information Der Deutschen Nationalbibliothek
Die Deutsche Nationalbibliothek verzeichnet diese Publikation in der Deutschen
Nationalbibliografie; detaillierte bibliografische Daten sind im Internet über
<http://dnb.ddb.de> abrufbar.

Original edition
© 2008 Psychosozial-Verlag
E-Mail: info@psychosozial-verlag.de
www.psychosozial-verlag.de
All rights reseved. No portion of this publication may be reproduced in any manner
without the written permission of the publisher.
Draft design cover: Atelier Warminski, Büdingen
Print layout: Hanspeter Ludwig, Gießen
ISBN 978-3-89806-780-5

Contents

Reviewers for this issue were:

Helen Resneck-Sannes
Maê Nascimento
Margit Koemeda-Lutz
Vincentia Schroeter

Letter from the Editor

You hold in your hands the 18th volume of the Clinical Journal of the International Institute for Bioenergetic Analysis. This issue represents current contributions in thinking emerging from the IIBA conference in Seville, Spain, which took place in May, 2007.

The trip to Spain was enriching both professionally and personally for me. Traveling for the first time from the USA to Spain I wanted to see if I could find any Spanish relatives from my mother's side of the family. Armed only with some 30 year old photos, two names of cousins, and knowledge that they had owned a bakery, my husband and I rented a car in Salamanca and drove to Peneranda Brocamonte. Behind that small town we found the little village of Mancera de Abajo, the birthplace of my grandparents, Mariano and Ceferina Sanchez. My mother had died a year before and I felt sadness and excitement stepping onto the earth where her grandfather herded sheep and her parents met and married. We parked right in front of the small town plaza where I had heard stories of my grandparents flirting over a hundred years ago. I had my husband take the photo of my first step onto this plaza, which appears on the cover of this issue. Later I did find cousins running a bakery. We shared stories and they enthusiastically welcomed us into their homes for a day of sharing and eating.

In Bioenergetics we speak much about grounding, the great concept introduced by our founder Alexander Lowen. That day, when I stepped onto the pebbles of that plaza, I found my Spanish roots, and as I walked around slowly, I felt grounded in the history of my heritage. Large raindrops slowly began to drop as we drove away that afternoon, joining with my tears of gratitude for such a moving experience. I called my Aunt in California, who was thrilled to hear I had found the town. It was she who had said, "If you ever find the village, please bring me back a pebble from that fine earth." I had a bag full of pebbles and joy in my heart, mixed with tears of missing Mom and at the same time feeling closer to her and fulfilled for finding my roots.

After our satisfying find of the hometown we traveled to Seville to join colleagues in a stimulating conference with a theme of addressing the place of Bioenergetics in today's world. Each day a keynote address reflected one of the themes. An emphasis on providing Bioenergetics to help the poor in social programs was illustrated by the Brazilian community, who inspired us to follow their lead by creating similar programs in our own countries.

In this volume we have four of the keynote addresses, one paper from a workshop, and two book reviews.

Guy Tonella created an ambitious project elaborating the development of new paradigms in psychotherapy, placing Bioenergetics within a larger context historically and theoretically. Guy's contribution here is part of an upcoming book he is writing. He also wants readers to know that his paper can be ordered directly from him in Spanish or French. All papers will be available in Portuguese, as the entire volume will be translated from English to Portuguese by one of our hardworking editors, Mae Nasciemento.

Garry Cockburn, with great respect for the legacy of Al Lowen uses contributions from philosophy to imagine an updated view of Bioenergetics without losing the value of the old concepts.

Angela Klopstech's keynote was an impassioned call for Bioenergetic therapists to use the language of modern psychotherapy and neuroscience to update our terms as a way of bringing Bioenergetics to other schools of psychology, and bringing them to us with a common way of speaking.

Ben Shapiro shares the highly creative development of a new technique he presented at the conference in a workshop. He generously provides the details and visuals of his "curling" technique, which is part of what he will include in a series of workbooks he is developing.

Scott Baum provides a paper from his keynote on the often understudied topic of the affect of fathers, in a style that is strongly argued, bravely personal, unique and stimulating.

Both Angela Klopstech and I are including book reviews in this volume. The book she reviews is only available in German, and the one I review is available in English.

I am including some business related to a previous journal, where Diana Guest has a comment about her paper published in volume 16: "I would like to make a belated acknowledgment of Paul Sussman, Ph.D. He and I were inspired by Bioenergetics and the writings of Jack Morin. We co-created a workshop and presented it at the Southern California Bioenergetics Conference in Feb. 2003. From there I went on to create and present an expanded version of our workshop at the Cape Cod IIBA conference in 2005 and write an article for the IIBA Journal that was published in 2006, "Bioenergetics and a Paradoxical View of Sexuality: how characterlogical development is related to current erotic life!" I regret that in that article I failed to acknowledge Paul's valuable contribution to that workshop we developed together which became the seed of my article that was published three years later. Thank you Paul. At this time I would also like to express my appreciation to all those who gave me support in a variety of ways. Thank you. Diana Guest"

I hope you all enjoy these stimulating articles. As for my first time sitting in the chief editor seat, I can say it has been a challenging task and a stimulating learning experience to create this journal, which I could not have completed without the steadfast mentoring of the previous chief editor, Margit Koemeda. I want to thank both her and Mae Nasciemento for being editors again with me. I also want to thank Helen Resneck-Sannes, who along with the three of us, gave of her time as a reviewer. Lastly I want to thank the authors who are providing us with the products of their creative ideas put down in a form for us to thoughtfully savor and enjoy.

Happy Reading!

Vincentia Schroeter, PhD, MFT, CBT
Encinitas, California, USA
November 7, 2007

Standing on both Legs: A Bioenergetic Perspective on the Family, Gender Roles and the Development of the Self in the 21st Century[1]

Garry Cockburn

Summary

How does Bioenergetics, which is focused on the body of the individual, articulate its concerns about the family and gender roles? And how can we add new ideas to Bioenergetics without betraying Alexander Lowen's essential ideas, whose integrity he strongly protected? The model of 'suspicion and recovery' of Paul Ricoeur, the French philosopher, allows us to discover what is unexamined, unexplored or repressed in Lowen's ideas on the body and the self. This hermeneutic perspective enables us to examine the *otherness of the embodied self* in a way that honors Lowen's genius and his emphasis on the body. It also provides a way to critique the historical limitations of Lowen's views on the development of the self, the family and gender roles, and provides a pathway for incorporating new knowledge into Bioenergetics.

Keywords: Hermeneutics, Otherness of the Embodied Self, Social Ethics

Introduction

My passion and difficulty in preparing this paper, has been to find a way of discussing the family, gender and development of the self, and yet, still be true to the essence of Bioenergetics. This has not been easy. Bioenergetics

---

1 Address given at IIBA International Conference at Seville, Spain, May, 2007.

was founded by Alexander Lowen to work with individuals, not families. So that is one basic problem.

Another is that Alexander Lowen once said, 'When I die, don't kill me!' (Sollmann, 2007, p. 1). Somehow or other, he knew that his followers might want to change the essence of his work, and thereby 'kill him'. When he was strong, he fought off these challenges. And yet, if we are to address today's issues, we must do this, even as Lowen did this to Reich.

When he came to write his first book, Lowen explicitly stated that Bioenergetics was independent of Reichian theory and techniques (Lowen, 1958, p. xii). He knew that it was considered heretical to question or modify any of Reich's concepts in the light of one's own experience, but he knew he must do that if he was to be true to himself and his creativity. (Lowen, 1975, p. 36).

Lowen's insight was to really look at and see bodily expression. He wrote:

> the next logical development of analysis was to look at the patient's body for an understanding of behavior… Being able to see and to understand bodily expression is what Bioenergetics is about. (Lowen, 2004, p. 99, p. 101).

The body was Lowen's passion, his life, from his first written words till his last. In the preface to his first book on the body he wrote:

> … Only with humility and candor dare one come face to face with the great wells of feeling which lie at the core of human beings. (Lowen, 1958, p. xii).

And in the last pages of his autobiography he says:

> I love the body. I love to work the body. I love to see the body blossom. That's my life.
> The body has always saved me. Fulfillment for me is living the life of the body and experiencing the energy of the body. The fulfillment that life and therapy offer is the ability to be fully true to one's self. That self for me is the bodily self, the only self we will ever know. Trust it, love it and be true to yourself. (Lowen, 2004, pp. 237–243).

I take this to be his last will and testament. And it is with gratitude that I accept this legacy. I am grateful also to Eleanor Greenlee[2], who first brought

---

2 Eleanor Greenlee, an IIBA faculty member, ran several workshops in NZ in 1989 and 1990.

Bioenergetics to New Zealand, to Ferrell Irvine[3] and the Bioenergetic trainers[4] who came to New Zealand to pass on his gifts.

And yet, there is a truth in the fact that we have to do what he feared – we do have 'to kill him off'. But here's the secret – we have to do that so that we can keep the essence of his work and his spirit alive, so that we can keep Bioenergetics fresh and creative. But we have do it in the right way, if that is to happen.

So what is the right way? This is a big problem. It is an issue that is at the heart of this Conference and which needs to be struggled with. I think some of us might be 'killing him off' on a daily basis with a thousand tiny cuts. If we just keep 'adding ideas' to Bioenergetics (e. g. intersubjectivity, post-structural feminism, neuroscience, trauma, attachment theory, etc.) we run the risk of losing our Bioenergetic identity by transforming ourselves into a generic 'catch-all' somatic psychotherapy. However, we also just as surely 'kill him off' when we treat his words and techniques as dogma, as unchanging truths that should not be questioned or changed. He, then, is in danger of becoming mummified, and we, of becoming irrelevant to today's world. So we have a dilemma.

The big question is, are these two ways our only choice: either to go wandering through the intellectual shopping malls, adding the latest ideas to our Bioenergetic baskets, or, on the other hand, to go on endlessly repeating the Lowenian past? What, then, is the proper relationship between tradition and innovation? How can we articulate the continuity between what we have received and new knowledge?

There is a third option. In order to establish this third way to keep Lowen's spirit alive, we need to detour into the hermeneutic tradition. The great French philosopher Paul Ricoeur, has given us the model of 'suspicion and recovery' (Ricoeur, 1970, pp. 32ff.). What he means by 'suspicion and recovery' is that in the writings of any genius, such as Freud or Marx, who have systematized their knowledge and who have a school of followers, we should 'suspect' that

---

3 In 1990, Ferrell Irvine emigrated from Chicago to New Zealand to set up a Bioenergetic training course. The NZ Society for Bioenergetic Analysis (NZSBA) owes its existence to Ferrell's courageous act.
4 Michael Maley, Eleanor Greenlee, Louise Fréchette, Bennett Shapiro, Helen Resneck-Sannes, Bob Hilton, Virginia Wink-Hilton and David Finlay. David lived in NZ for more than three years assisting NZSBA.

there is a depth of unexplored, unexamined or even repressed meaning, and that this deeper meaning can and must be 'recovered' by a critical analysis of their work.

It may well be that Lowen has left key concepts unexamined and unexplored, perhaps even repressed, in order to get his ideas across. So that one way of going forward is to 'suspect' that *all the meaning* has not been fully extracted from Lowen's basic ideas on the body and the self. If this were so, and we were able to 'recover' deeper meanings that lay within, we may yet be able to keep the genius of Lowen alive and fresh. At the same time we would be able to maintain the relevance of Bioenergetic Analysis as the world's largest school of somatic psychotherapy.

I have called this paper, 'Standing on Both Legs'. For the purposes of the Conference theme[5] I am going to make the suggestion that the 1st leg of Bioenergetics be the *somatic* understanding of *oneself, as an individual*. All of Lowen's work was dedicated to this task. Now I am going to make the bold suggestion that the 2nd leg of Bioenergetics be the *somatic* understanding of *oneself, in relationship to the other*[6].

This would mean finding a way, if there was one, of bringing *the other*, (or relationality, or intersubjectivity) into the central theory, practice and research of Bioenergetics. In preparing this paper it has become evident that we are not able to fully understand the development of the self, gender issues and the family in the 21st century without this 2nd leg of Bioenergetics. In this paper, I want to develop this idea, the idea of the *otherness of the embodied self*. We will look at the development of the self, and then at gender issues and the family, all from this point of view.

Development of the Self

Let us start with the development of the self, as this is foundational to everything else. Remember what Lowen said, '*that self for me is the bodily self, the only self we will ever know*'. He defined the essence of Bioenergetics as being able *to look at* the body and *to see and to understand bodily expression*,

---

5 IIBA 2007 Conference theme: Self & Community – Creating Connections in Broken Times.
6 This phrase reflects the title of Ricoeur's book (1990) 'Oneself as Another'.

and he developed the brilliant techniques that we have all inherited for that purpose.

So how does Lowen account for the development of the self? Just as we are trying to do, to find what remains unexplored or unexamined in Lowen, Lowen himself delighted in bringing out the deeper meaning in Freud's early statement, that 'the ego is first and foremost a body ego' (Lowen, 1958, p. 19). For Lowen, his fundamental thesis is that the origin of the self arises from the physical bio-energy in the body. This physical bio-energy is expressed in both psychic phenomena and in somatic movement. And, as he has so brilliantly pointed out, it is the dialectical relationship between psyche and soma, or, mind and body, at the different developmental stages that gives rise to the different character structures.

Although Lowen and Reich were not formally trained in philosophy, this dialectical view of psyche and soma in the development of the self, places them firmly in a European philosophical tradition, starting from Hegel. For Hegel, however, the self is essentially 'intersubjective'. It knows itself only if it recognizes the equal and independent reality of others, and only if others recognize the equal and independent reality of the self (Beiser, 2005, p. 177). This was in stark contrast to Descartes, *Cogito ergo sum* – *I think therefore I am,* which asserts that the self knows itself independently of others and the world.

Despite this Hegelian inheritance, there is no mention in *The Language of the Body,* Lowen's major work, that *the other,* or intersubjectivity, is *a constitutive part* of the bodily self. The important dialectical relationship is between psyche and soma, and never, not even for one instance, between mother and baby[7]. It is almost as if Lowen has reverted to a Cartesian position of *corpus ergo sum* – *I am a body therefore I am,* that the bodily self knows itself independently of others and the world.

Lowen is one third of the way through *The Language of the Body* before he mentions that the individual has a mother. Then the infant is not talked about in an active or interactive manner, but in the passive tense, e. g. *'the infant has already been subjected to a vital experience of nine month's duration', 'Infants born from these wombs will differ'.* There is only one sentence in the whole of this book that talks about the effects of good mother-love

---

7 For an elaboration of the dialectical relationship between mother/child refer Ogden (1990, 1996).

on the body and mind of the individual, and this is done in a one-directional and rather abstract manner: *'the development that takes place under optimum conditions produces a body structure and personality which evokes our admiration'*. (Lowen, 1958, p. 109).

Of course, Lowen is well aware of the interactive relationship between mother and child. He gives multiple examples in his writings[8], and he often refers to his own mother's cruel yet seductive relationship with himself. The key Lowenian principle is that the manner and quality of standing on one's feet is dependent on the energy and support one's mother gave in the earliest years (Lowen, 2004, p. 135). While the parental/child interactions of the Oedipal complex are expounded at length in *Fear of Life* and *Love and Orgasm*, his most extensive account of the preoedipal mother/child relationship is in *Betrayal of the Body,* (Lowen, 1967, pp. 189–208) his book on the schizoid condition. This makes grim reading. His negative description of these mothers hardly privileges the mother/baby relationship as we now know we must.

So what might be *unexamined, what unexplored, what might be repressed* in Lowen's view of the development of the self? What seems unexamined is the reality that *otherness* or intersubjectivity is built-in to the body and to the self. This is fundamental! *Otherness* is built-in to the body and the self. *Otherness* is built-in biologically, dialectically, ethically, neurologically, ontologically, psychically, sexually, socially, somatically and spiritually. It is built-in to the very nature of the bodily self.

Paul Ricoeur, like Lowen, asserts the primacy of the body in understanding the self. But Ricoeur, unlike Lowen, asserts that *otherness is not added on to selfhood from the outside*. It is a constitutive part of the self's very being and meaning (Ricoeur, 1992, pp. 317ff.).

For Ricoeur, it is through my body, that I am aware that I am in the world, that I exist, and that I can want, I can move and I can act. This is a foundational human experience. My body is the bridge to reality. Secondly, I am aware that others, over there, are foreign to me, that they can nurture me or hurt me, and that I, through my body, can be open to them or resist them. Through my body I exist among others, I exist intersubjectively.

---

8 Lowen (1965) Love and Orgasm. pp. 33–46. Lowen (1975a) Pleasure. pp. 84ff. Lowen (1972) Depression and the Body. pp. 129ff. Lowen (1975) Bioenergetics. pp. 111ff. Lowen (1980) Fear of Life. pp. 24ff; pp59ff; pp. 160ff. Lowen (1985) Narcissism. p. 12; pp. 188ff. Lowen (1988) Love, Sex and your Heart. pp. 50ff. Lowen (2004) Honoring the Body. p. 145.

Ricoeur adds a third level of meaning that arises from the otherness of the body, which we will examine later when examining the family and the social implications of Bioenergetics. It is through my body I am aware that I should not hurt others in their bodily selves. Through the otherness of my body '*I wish to live well, with and for others in just institutions*' (Ricoeur, 1992. pp. 341ff.).

For Ricoeur, then, the *otherness of the body* gives rise to our three greatest experiences at the level of meaning: my experience of my own body, my experience of others, and my experience that I wish to live with and for others – that I have an ethical conscience (Ricoeur, 1992, p. 318).

Lowen, does not seem to have explored or examined this deep otherness of the body. He may, in actual fact, have *repressed* it. Helen Resneck-Sannes (2005, p. 42) has drawn attention to Lowen's account, in his book *Bioenergetics*, of the breakdown of his therapy with Reich. It had taken Lowen over 100 sessions to get to the meaning of the scream he discovered in his very first session with Reich. This scream was his terror as a baby looking into his mother's rageful eyes[9]. Following Reich's failure to respond to Lowen in the nurturing way he wanted, Lowen said he felt 'doomed'.

It was after this that Lowen started developing Bioenergetics through his work with Pierrakos. Note what Lowen says:

> (My therapy) had an entirely different quality from my work with Reich. There were fewer of the spontaneously moving experiences.... This was mainly because I largely directed the body work.... In the first half of the session I worked with myself, describing my bodily sensations to Pierrakos. In the second half, he dug in on my tight muscles.... Working on myself, I developed the basic positions and exercises which are now standard in bioenergetics.... I began in a standing position rather than the prone one Reich used. (Lowen, 1975, p. 39).

This is not a *relational* therapy he is developing. He says, 'I largely directed the body work.... Working on myself, I developed the basic positions. I began in a standing position rather than the prone one Reich used'.

Lowen gives another account of this work with Pierrakos. It was probably written about the same time as the quote from the book *Bioenergetics*.

---

9 Note also Lowen's other account of this terrorized scream in Lowen (1996) Keynote Address in Bioenergetic Analysis. The Clinical Journal of the IIBA. 7 (1) 3 &10–11.

... we began this therapy with me in the standing position rather than lying down... The two positions, lying and standing, reflect two different ways of being in the world. In the lying down position one adopts by implication an infantile mode; being on one's back denotes helplessness. This position favors regression and facilitates the recall of early memories and experiences. Standing on one's feet denotes an adult posture and furthers the processes leading to maturity and responsibility. (Lowen, 1976, p. 41).

Philip Helfaer (1998, p. 47) has noted that getting people off the couch and onto their feet was a symbolic break with the whole European analytic tradition. David Boadella has called Bioenergetics, *The Active Method* (1990, p. 16) with its emphasis on working with the oedipal complex (1985, p. 13) and with a body that is already on its feet. By rising above the *helplessness* of the baby, Lowen took a profound strategic stance that affects us today. While this focus on 'standing' moved Lowen away from his terrorizing mother, it also moved Bioenergetics away from the earliest experiences of body and self in relationship, and away from the primary ground where 'oneself also includes the other'[10].

I believe, by affirming with Ricoeur, that *otherness is not added onto the body from the outside*, that we can then incorporate Ricoeur's philosophical idea of the *otherness of the body* with Lowen's privileging of the body. In doing so we would create a strong theoretical basis for a two-person therapy (Stark, 1999; Klopstech, 2002) within modern Bioenergetics.

Gender Issues

It is from this position of 'otherness' that we can now take a brief look at Lowen's position on gender and the family. In respect of gender, we know that some of Lowen's ideas on women and homosexuality are difficult to deal with. These statements were, as he says (Lowen 1962, p. 196, pp. 237ff.), 'not

---

10 Note Lowen's (1995, p. 2) revealing statement that he has 'accepted the fact that I do not need to be loved...and not dependent on another'. Refer also Lowen's (2004, p. 217) comments: 'This need to prove my superiority stemmed from a deep feeling of humiliation associated with my bodily functions and from my identification with my mother in her contempt for the body. Although my therapy with Reich lessened this identification with my mother, it did not ground me enough in my body'.

definitive statements' and were reflective of his clinical experiences and the gender hierarchies prevalent in New York in the 1950's.

> In our culture there appears to be a reversal of values. Feminine values have gained the ascendancy. I believe that the loss of manhood is related somehow to this reversal of values, to the fact that men have taken on themselves the drudgery of life.

and

> Probably because of the turning inward and lack of sharp focus in her body, the woman needs the man or his image to produce a strong genital excitement. Man is women's bridge to the world.

Contrast this with Maori New Zealanders' view of the relationship between the sexes as revealed in the following myth. *Maui*, the great Polynesian male hero, wanted to find out the deepest secrets of life. To learn the secrets of the underworld, he entered the vagina of the sleeping giantess, *Hine Nui Te Po*, the Great Mother of the Night. As he was re-emerging at daybreak the sleeping giantess awoke, and *Maui* got crushed to death in her toothed vagina. Even today, at ritual ceremonies, if a Maori man gets too big for his boots, Maori women will turn their backs on him, bend over and raise their skirts[11], reminding him where all men have come from (Salmond, 1975, p. 151).

As long as thirty years ago, Bioenergetic women disagreed with Lowen's theories as they applied to women's sexuality. In response to a research questionnaire from Alice and Harold Ladas (1981), 87% of women disagreed with Lowen, even though over 80% of them had reported improvements to their sexual lives as a result of Bioenergetics. Evidently Lowen was not impressed by this 'raising of skirts' by our Bioenergetic women. Similar research today would likely result in a higher percentage of women disagreeing, and an even higher percentage of us disagreeing with his views on homosexuality.

> Homosexuality is an unconscious attempt to establish a heterosexual relationship... one finds that the homosexual is usually emotionally deadened.... Male homosexuality has its origin in an incestuous relationship with the mother. (Lowen, 1962, pp. 195ff.).

---

11 This derisory practice is called 'whakapohane' in Maori. (Literally: *to act in a ridiculous manner*).

Clearly, we have some urgent updating to do on homosexuality, gender development and gender hierarchies. While this may mean challenging the traditional Freudian and Lowenian position that gender is set at the oedipal stage, it does not necessarily mean a major departure from Lowen's position, as he does point out that:

> the events in the preoedipal period from birth to three years of age are equally important (as the oedipal stage) in shaping character, though they do not determine its final form. (Lowen, 1980, p. 160).

Note however, that he is talking about character, not gender.

In fact, modern feminist psychoanalytic studies are giving much more attention to the *preoedipal* aspect of gender development, and in doing so, are creating the conditions for a multiplicity of gender outcomes. For instance feminist writers are referring to the maternal body as the locus of excitement for all offspring, not just male children.

This emphasis on the maternal is balanced by what happens at the rapprochement stage. Jessica Benjamin (1998, p. 61) suggests that all children have a love affair with the father who represents the exciting, compelling outside world; he is the figure of freedom who has access to and enjoys the world.

Benjamin (1998) also balances the traditional Freudian father-centered oedipal model with an emphasis on the mother's contribution to our subjectivity, deepest desires and gender identity. This emphasis on the mother and on women's sexuality links us directly back to the body, back to the essential otherness of the woman's body, separate to and equal with the man's body. This does not demean the role of men and male sexuality. In fact, it frees men up from the patriarchal burden of the classical oedipal situation. It allows them to have both their hearts and their balls.

Thus if we incorporate *the other* as part of the engendered self from the earliest moments, we might then start to see the subtle intersubjective gender complexities that occur both *before and after* the oedipal stage is reached. And, in doing this, we might avoid stereotypical gender models, which are stuck in the binary choice of either male or female as set at the oedipal stage. We might then well find we have a more satisfactory answer, to the multitude of gender variations, including homosexuality, that make up gender difference in the 21st century.

Although Lowen's early statements on gender are no longer acceptable, it is important to recognize that his primary emphasis on the body, like Ricoeur's, is in fact, also a philosophical statement. Much early radical feminist literature was based on the post-structural position that gender is entirely a cultural construct, and that the self is de-centered and nothing but the outcome of language. Our challenge is to take on board the legitimate criticisms of strong feminists without losing contact with the reality of the bodily self, Lowen's enduring gift to Bioenergetics.

Family

Despite massive changes to the Western family, which we are all aware of, the family remains vitally important as the fundamental source of emotional, physical and financial care and support for most people (NZ Department of Statistics, 2006).

When Lowen talks about his own family he shares a surprising amount of intimate details about his parents and his early family life, about his sexual life, and about his relationship with his wife. He also shares a surprising amount about his negative relationship with his other family – us, the IIBA.

We know from his writing (Lowen, 2004, p. 54) that his wife, Leslie, was 'his other', the person, he said, who balanced his intellectualism and his difficulty in accessing feelings. While they were working together in Hawaii, on the island of *Maui*, (remember *Maui*) Lowen tells us he triggered Leslie's rage by intruding into her work with a man whose inflated chest Lowen thought was blocking his sadness for his unhappy mother. Lowen (2004, p. 179) tells us that he left the room feeling dejected. He said, '*I have never forgotten that incident and never will*'.

It may be that the sight of Leslie working with a man who seemed to carry his mother's pain was a bit too close to Lowen's own pain[12]. Lowen (2004, p. 92) has said:

> I have long believed that the role of the therapist has something to do with a deep need, conscious or unconscious, to save one's mother... I sensed this was true of me... As a child, I sensed her pain, although I refused to carry her burden. However I could not close my eyes to her suffering.

---

12 Lowen (2004, p. 134) stated that: 'He (Reich) had perceived quickly that I was holding my chest in an inflated position which he knew was an expression of fear.'

If Lowen had opened his eyes and his heart to *his own suffering* about his rageful mother, then Bioenergetics may well have developed differently[13]. As has been noted, that first contact of the embodied self with the other, with *M-other,* is the foundation for all later developments. Without this basis in the feminine, we in Bioenergetics do not have an effective way of understanding the dynamics of the family. We know from developmental studies that the baby is held, firstly in the matrix of the mother's womb, then in her arms, eyes and breasts, and then in the matrix of the mother and father – the family.

Basing Bioenergetics firmly in this sequential relational matrix gives us a way of working with the family. We can help young adults heal their wounding from their earliest years, confirm the gender patterning that suits them so that their sexuality can be expressed and fully shared with their chosen mate. And we can support them to become parents who raise the next generation in a manner that allows their children a true childhood.

Lowen also has a more sociological way of looking at the family. However, his approach is a straightforward reflection of Reich's analysis of the patriarchal nature and power-relationships within Western families.

> The family, as Wilhelm Reich has pointed out, is the operative agent of society (1975a, p. 67).... In most families, the training for this life style starts early in the life of the child (1980, p. 38)... I have come to realise that my family situation was not as unique as I once thought... Why?The patriarchal order is a vertical hierarchy... with the father at the top, the mother below him and the children at the bottom (1980, pp. 197ff.).

In respect of this wider Reichian perspective on the family, it is important to realise that Reich, as a Marxist, said that you could not develop a sociological theory of the family out of psychological ideas (Reich, 1972, pp. 59ff.). He therefore went outside of psychoanalysis to help him understand the family. Reich used sociological and cultural perspectives (Boadella, 1985, p. 68) as the basis for his social action to help liberate women, young people and the family. Although Lowen (2004, p. 92) said that he was *'not a revolutionary like Reich'* he does have a broad vision:

---

13 On the other hand, we may not have inherited Lowen's genius to see the body if he had understood his pain in 'relational' terms.

Our task is to understand human nature and to influence cultural patterns so that they favor this nature (Lowen, 1976, p. 48)

While he was well aware of Reich's socio/political perspective, Lowen did not, himself, develop an explicit sociological or cultural perspective like Reich, and did not become a social activist. However his profound insights into the body did empower his *'sincere hope that he would help alleviate the sufferings of people'*. (Lowen, 1976, p. 48).

Bioenergetics does have trouble in formulating a socio/political ethic in respect of families and the wider society because of Lowen's individualistic bias. But contrary to Reich's Marxist position, a social perspective can be developed out of psychological ideas by privileging the body as containing both 'self and other'. As Paul Ricoeur (1992, pp. 317ff.) has pointed out, the otherness of the body links us intimately with all other people in a spirit of mutuality and respect. We do have a deep wish to live well with and for others in just institutions.

Just how Bioenergetics develops a social ethic is a challenge that besets us all, and gives rise to many more questions than answers. Two of those questions might be: how do we provide somatic psychotherapy for less-well-off individuals and families in our societies and, how do we integrate into our theory, practice and research, the social-cultural, political and environmental issues that affect individuals and families?

Lowen's injunction that our task is *'to influence cultural patterns'* does not mean that we should become crusading rock-stars or social workers. Most of us are, and will remain, therapists to individuals. But it does mean that we each embody an ethical, social and political 'instinct' in our work, 'an alertness on when we must do good'[14] (Ogden, 2005, p. 22), whether it be helping an individual to become a better person in their family and community, or, in fact, helping the disadvantaged in a social clinic in Brazil.

The real implications of incorporating *the other* into the embodied self remain to be fully worked out. That task belongs to us all. However, in closing, it is important to acknowledge the work that has already been done by our own relational theory builders, and the work that has already been done in developing a social ethic for Bioenergetics by our South American colleagues.

---

14 A quote from Borges.

Some key references are: Hilton (1996, 2003), Finlay (1999), Klopstech (2000, 2000a), Tonella (2000), Lewis (2005), Resneck-Sannes (2005), Weigand (2006), Trucillo (2006), Correia et al. (1999).

Conclusion

To conclude, we are a family from across the globe, with a plurality of differences that enrich us all. Our own *otherness* is reflected in the IIBA. We have seen how many of Lowen's views reflect his own psychology and his historical location in New York. We need not be over-determined by that history or by his individualist viewpoint. But we can never be over-determined by Alexander Lowen's love of the body. That is fundamental to our Bioenergetic identity.

We have been given a great gift by Alexander Lowen. He created a powerful and original way of seeing the body. He loved the body, he loved to see the body blossom. That was his life. His last published words were about the bodily self. '*Trust it, love it and be true to yourself*'.

We must keep true to Lowen's focus on the embodied self, and yet we must be true to ourselves and to the future of Bioenergetics. One of the ways we can do that is by bringing out some of the deeper meanings embedded in his work, and by continuing to develop the implications of the *otherness of the embodied self*.

But most of all, we can finally incorporate the *helplessness* of the baby (Lowen, 1976, p. 41) and in doing so, find the energy to stand as grounded *adults* on both legs. And that is how we keep the essence of Alexander Lowen's work and his spirit alive.

References

Beiser F (2005) Hegel. Routledge, New York.
Benjamin J (1998) Shadow of the Other. Routledge, New York.
Boadella D (1985) Wilhelm Reich: The Evolution of His Work. Arkana, London.
Boadella D (1990) Somatic Psychotherapy: Its Roots and Traditions. In: Energy and Character 21 (1) 2–26.
Correia G, Alves J, Rapela A, Araujo L (1999) Bioenergetics Applied to Social Clinics. Bioenergetic Analysis 10 (1) 45–52.
Finlay D (1999) A Relational Approach to Bioenergetics. Bioenergetic Analysis 10 (2) 35–52.

Helfaer P (1976) Sex and Self Respect. Praeger Publishers, Westport, CT.

Hilton R (1996) The Recovery of Self and the client/therapist Relationship. Bioenergetic Analysis 7 (1) 90–101.

Hilton R (2003) The Importance of Relationship in Bioenergetic Analysis. The European J. of Bioenergetic Analysis and Psychotherapy 1 (1) 32–45.

Klopstech A (2000) The Bioenergetic Use of a Psychoanalytic Conception of Cure. Bioenergetic Analysis 11 (1) 43–54.

Klopstech A (2000a) Psychoanalysis and Body Psychotherapies. Bioenergetic Analysis 11 (1) 55–66.

Ladas A K & Ladas H (1981) Women and Bioenergetic Analysis. Connecticut Society for Bioenergetic Analysis.

Lewis R (2005) The Anatomy of Empathy. Bioenergetic Analysis 15 9–31.

Lowen A (1958) Language of the Body. Macmillan Publishing Co., New York.

Lowen A (1962) Sex and Personality. In: Lowen A (2005) The Voice of the Body. Bioenergetic Press, Florida.

Lowen A (1965) Love and Orgasm. Macmillan Publishing Co., New York.

Lowen A (1967) The Betrayal of the Body. Macmillan Publishing Co., New York.

Lowen A (1972) Depression and the Body. Penguin, New York.

Lowen A (1975) Bioenergetics. Penguin Books, New York.

Lowen A (1975a) Pleasure: a Creative Approach to Life. Penguin Books, New York.

Lowen A (1976) Reich, sex and orgasm. In: Boadella D ed. (1976) In the Wake of Reich. Coventure Ltd., London.

Lowen A (1980) Fear of Life. Macmillan Publishing Co., New York.

Lowen A (1980a) Stress and Illness. In: Lowen A (2005) The Voice of the Body. Bioenergetic Press, Florida.

Lowen A (1985) Narcissism: Denial of the True Self. Macmillan Publishing Co., New York.

Lowen A (1988) Love Sex & Your Heart. Macmillan Publishing Co., New York.

Lowen A (1995) The Process of Bioenergetic Analysis. Bioenergetic Analysis 6 (1) 2.

Lowen A (1996) Keynote Address. Bioenergetic Analysis 7 (1) 3–11.

Lowen A (2004) Honoring the Body. Bioenergetic Press, Florida.

New Zealand Department of Statistics (2006) Report: International Developments in Family Statistics (2006). <www.stats.govt.nz>. Website accessed November 2006.

Ogden T (1990) The Matrix of the Mind. Jason Aronson, Northvale, NJ.

Ogden T (1996) Subjects of Analysis. Jason Aronson, Northvale, NJ.

Ogden T (2005) This Art of Psychoanalysis. Routledge, New York.

Salmond A (1975) Hui. Reed, Wellington.

Sollmann U (2007) We are our own client – encounter the organisation. First published in English on IIBA website in March 2007.

Stark M (1999) Modes of Therapeutic Action. Jason Aronson, Northvale, NJ.

Tonella G (2000) The Interactive Self/Le Soi Interactif. Bioenergetic Analysis 11 (2) 25–59.

Resneck-Sannes H (2005) Bioenergetics: Past, Present and Future. Bioenergetic Analysis 15 33–54.

Ricoeur P (1970) Freud and Philosophy: An Essay on Interpretation. Yale Uni. Press, New Haven.

Ricoeur P (1990) Oneself as Another. Uni. of Chicago Press. Chicago.

Reich W (1972) Dialectical Materialism and Psychoanalysis. In: Baxandall L ed. (1972) Sex-Pol: Essays, 1929–1934 Wilhelm Reich.

Trucillo E (2006) A Somatopsychic Relational Model for Growing an Emotionally Healthy, Sexually Open Body from the Ground Up. Bioenergetic Analysis 16 63–86.

Weigand O (2006) Grounding e Autonomia: A Terapia Corporal Bioenergética Revisitada. Person, Sao Paulo.

About the Author

Garry Cockburn BSW(Hons)., CBT., was born in New Zealand, trained as a Catholic priest in Sydney, Australia in the 1960s, and then undertook postgraduate studies in theology in Rome. After leaving the priesthood, he qualified as a social worker and worked in the New Zealand Government child abuse agency for nearly 30 years. He has worked as a social work consultant in the field of child abuse and child, adolescent and family mental health. He has published on the topic of a phenomenological approach to child protection legislation in New Zealand. He finished his Bioenergetic training in 1995, and is in private practice as a Bioenergetic psychotherapist with his partner, Pye Bowden, in their business, Mind & Body.

Garry Cockburn, BSW(Hons). CBT.
122 Maida Vale Rd
Roseneath
Wellington
New Zealand
garry.cockburn@paradise.net.nz

Paradigms for Bioenergetic Analysis At the dawn of the 21st Century

Guy Tonella

Summary

First, basic Lowenian paradigms are first reviewed, followed by updated bioenergetic paradigms, integrating contemporary theoretical and clinical contributions, articulated around the concept of Self:
➢ adaptive motility
➢ sexual motility
➢ motility of attachment

Three methodologies are distinguished:
➢ working on conflicts
➢ working on deficits
➢ working on traumas

Therapeutic intersubjective relationship is distinguished from analytical relationship. A developmental model from these up-dated bioenergetic paradigms is proposed. Lastly, a sociological approach is outlined as development of bioenergetic technique in a perspective of a "shared world".

Keywords: Bioenergetic Analysis, Paradigms, Self, Attachment, Intersubjective

Introduction

When he founded bioenergetic analysis half century ago, Lowen initiated a movement of a great amplitude. His personal charisma was an important factor. He also benefited from a vast sociological movement, in the Western hemisphere, that was seeking body experiences, expression and freedom. Back in those days, the hippie era was in full swing, all kinds of personal growth experiences were being made at Esalen, the development of humanistic psychology, a "vitalistic" orientation in psychotherapy was picking up speed. Bioenergetic Analysis was moving at the same time towards international expansion. It was seen as a form of psychotherapy, but it was also considered to be a preventive approach and a way to foster healthy life habits, in particular through "bioenergetic exercises".

But what is happening today?

The "need for vitality" is still strong. But in our contemporary world, where brain imagery graphically reveals healthy vs. pathological processes, we, bioenergetic therapists, must demonstrate the relevance of our therapeutic practices. Lowen was not inclined to promote scientific research. He once wrote to me: "There is no need to justify: clinical proofs are enough". Often times, the perception people from outside have about Bioenergetic Analysis is a simplistic one: "crying, hitting, screaming".

We all know that Bioenergetic Analysis is much more than that and we must continue to build from the legacy of its creator:

we must modernize or actualize its basic concepts while taking into account the present state of scientific research in the fields of neurobiology and psychophysiology; we must integrate in our reflection the various developmental theories of the child and the adult that have been clinically and experimentally confirmed; We must take into account the evolution of psychopathologies and the necessary evolution of Bioenergetic Analysis methodologies: We must take into account the evolution of the needs of our populations with regards to public health, while knowing that sociological and geopolitical contexts marked by growing problems of violence and social inequities demand that we become creative, which may mean getting out of our offices. Our Brazilian members are proposing stimulating models with regards to that.

At the dawn of this 21st century, all of this demands of us that we stimulate an adjustment of our paradigms, a renewal of our Bioenergetic Analysis theoretical model. Our credibility, our *"readability"* *(Note of the Translator: „readability" in the sense of „aptitude to be understood by others")*, as well as our efficiency is on the line. But even more important than that, it is the very identity of Bioenergetic Analysis that is at stake, that on which we found our common identity, that which enables us to see ourselves as bioenergetic therapists and that which gives the International Institute for Bioenergetic Analysis a shared meaning.

Our Heritage: Basic Paradigms in Bioenergetic Analysis

I would like to underline the essential paradigms Lowen bequeathed to us as a model for bioenergetic analysis. They are the majors concepts (theory) defining the clinical models (therapeutic practice). They are those that I learnt during my training (1978–1981).

Paradigm 1: psychosomatic functional identity

In "the Language of the Body" (1958), Lowen reaffirms the paradigm "of psychosomatic functional identity", as stated by Reich:

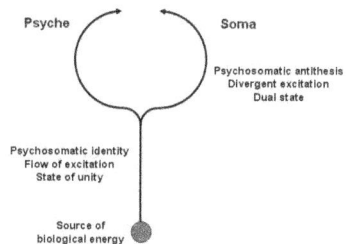

1) *The biological aspect* is: energy is the *functional* common denominator for psyche and for soma;

2) *The defensive aspect* is: when energy is blocked, it is by two *functionally* identical mechanisms: muscular tension and rejection of the neurotic psychic representations;

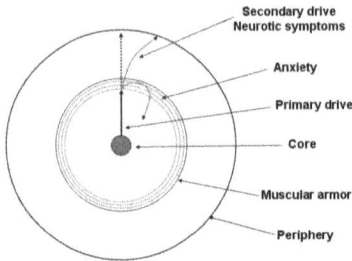

3) *The clinical aspect* is: these two mechanisms *functionally* inhibit emotional expression.

Paradigm 2: the Self is a mind-body continuity

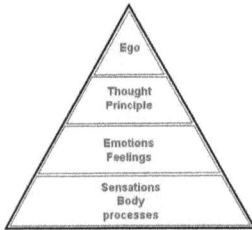

In his first monographs, Lowen uses the concept of Self (1965, 1968). He uses it again in "Narcissism" (1985). The Self is defined in terms of psychosomatic continuum: it includes the body experiences (feelings, emotions, movements) and the psychic experiences (perceptions, images, representations). He says, "we have a dual relationship with our body. We can have direct experience through our feelings or we can have an image of it" (pp. 29–30). Self is defined as mind-body continuum.

Paradigm 3: finality of the Self is spontaneous expressivity

Lowen based the practice of bioenergetic analysis on the awakening of self-awareness: through motility, movement and expression. In one of its first monographs (1965) Lowen comments: "The self-awareness means (…) to feel the flow of feelings which joins the fact of breathing. While passing in the body, respiratory waves activate all the muscular system (…). Being entirely alive means to breathe deeply, move freely and feel fully". The expressivity of oneself is related to a person's degree of energetic charge.

Paradigm 4: the therapeutic model is character analysis

Spontaneous processes can be blocked. In Bioenergetics (1975), Lowen clarifies the pathogenic diagram: "Lead to pleasure à privation/frustration à anxiety à defensive reaction". He adds: "It is a general outline explaining all the problems of personality" (p. 120). The sexual etiology of problems of personality is posed as well as the therapeutic method: freeing the repressed sexual instincts being opposed to vitality, expression and pleasure, by releasing muscular tensions which are at the origin".

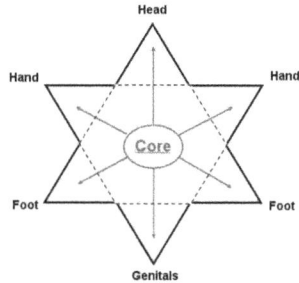

This method is called *character analysis* which combines verbal and body processes:
1) body process in order to release the muscular tensions,
2) verbal process in order to understand the significance of the representations at the origin of the conflict.

Reformulation of the paradigms and new paradigms

I will try to formulate those paradigms in a language that would not be understandable only within our bioenergetic community, but also understandable and attractive for our colleagues from other analytical and psychotherapeutic fields, for our colleagues from Universities, and for researchers. I believe that doing this effort is essential if we seek a new expansion at the dawn of this 21ˢᵗ century:
1) Reformulation of the concept of Self: this concept is still relevant and is shared by almost all psychotherapeutic approaches;
2) Reformulation of the energetic dynamics of the Self: his adaptive motility, his sexual motility and his attachment motility;
3) Formulation of the working methodology of traumas differentiated from the methodology of character analysis;
4) Formulation of a therapeutic relationship model giving a major role to the psychotherapist's intersubjective involvement;

5) Finally, I will propose a sociological paradigm for bioenergetic analysis, based on the principle of *shared vitality* for a *shared world*.

Paradigm I: The Self, a Body-mind Continuum

THE SELF AS AN INTERFACE

The Self is an interface between the biological and the social. It is built with cross biological processes which substantiate it and interpersonal processes which make it subjective. The Self is the phenomenological place of convergence between instinctual and sociocultural phenomena.

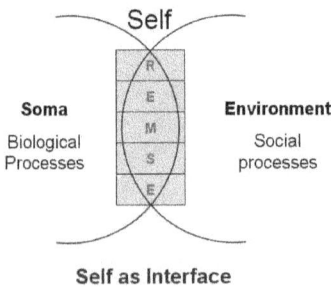

Self as Interface

The bodily Self is the first manifestation of the emerging Self. It is the first subjective reality of the Self and the foundation of development.

For example, the infant's sleep regulation as well as his feeding, physical and emotional expression regulation, are immediately subjected, on the one hand, to hereditary neurological mechanisms, and on the other hand, to the subjective social norms of his/her parents.

Blake (2002) shows that, conversely, these first social modelling modify neurobiological somatic processes: they cause structural and functional changes in neuronal connections. Concretely, the emotional experience modifies hippocampus cells, most sensitive to the emotional experiences, and they improve the effectiveness of synapses. On the other hand, working with attachment modifies fronto-limbic circuits, implicated in the patterning of

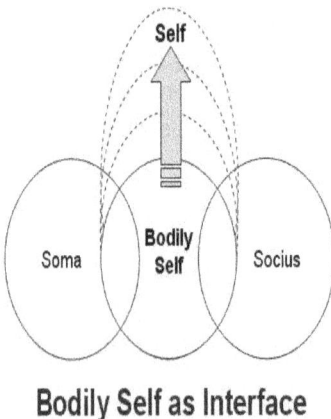

Bodily Self as Interface

"sensitivity". As Jeannerod (2005) demonstrates, this stimulates the emergence of new behaviours. For Kandel (2001), this constitutes the permanent dialectical process of exchange between soma and social, stimulating the neuronal "plasticity", that is, in its turn, transformative of the Self.

We, bioenergetic therapists, are specifically dealing with the patient's bodily Self. This bodily Self is an energetic reservoir where instincts are transformed into socialized, regulated drives which are the source of motility.

FUNCTIONS OF THE SELF

So, how to redefine the concept of Self? The Self is defined as a functional whole made of the co-integration of five *functions*: the energetic function, the sensory function, the motor function, the emotional function and the function of perception/representation.

Each function of the Self supports the other. The variations which occur in one of the functions of the Self cause variations in the whole, like a moving wave.

The energetic function is the seat of quantitative variations in excitation. Those variations stimulate the motility and vitality of the Self, through pulsations and vibrations. The modulation of energy flows produces phenomena of activation/deactivation. They are regulated by biological needs and patterned by family environment.

The Self, its Functions

The sensory function, through its qualitative manifestations, plays the role of primitive consciousness. Its expression is regulated and modelled by the family environment: for example, both pain and pleasure are subjected from the start to an expressive, approving/disapproving regulation.

The motor function has a double function. Through the adjustments of postural tone, it gives the Self the sensation of having a "tonic envelope" or conscious "boundary". Through the adjustments of its muscle tone, it prepares the Self for action and expression. Motor function supports the construction

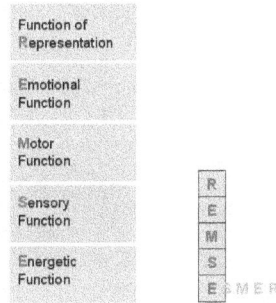

of patterns of action as well as postural patterns specific to a person, which are both shaped by interpersonal interactions.

The emotional function plays a role in expression and subjective communication with the social environment. Through its emotional bodily manifestations, it plays a cathartic role in the regulation of the Self. Through its affects, it contributes to the psychic elaboration of cognitive information.

The function of representation, through its system made of images and linguistic signs, gives a meaning to the energetic, sensory, motor and emotional experiences. It encodes and symbolizes them, making them communicable. It ensures the capacity of the Self to think and reflect upon oneself.

Each of these functions participates in self-consciousness, from the most elementary level (vital sensation of physical existence) to the most complex level (awareness of having a spirit of one's own). However, the integration of the Self depends upon the links that are built between those functions.

THE LINKS BETWEEN THE FUNCTIONS OF THE SELF

The first half of the 20th century opened up a new fields of research, which brought clarity to the specificity of each one of the links connecting each of these functions, as well as their process of "subjectivation" (*process by which the experience becomes subjective*): Freud (1887–1902; 1915a; 1915b; 1926), for the link between affect and representation; Reich (1933) and Wallon (1934), for the link between emotion and motor function; Piaget (1936) for the link between motor function and sensation and Lowen (1965, 1968, 1975, 1985) for the link between sensation and energy.

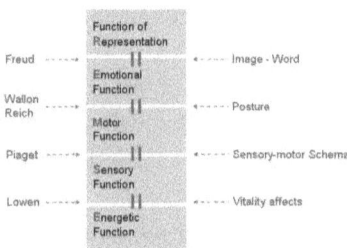

Freud	Function of Representation	Image - Word
Wallon / Reich	Emotional Function	Posture
Piaget	Motor Function	Sensory-motor Schema
Lowen	Sensory Function	Vitality affects
	Energetic Function	

The Self, its Function and its Links

The link Self – ground – constitutes a primitive system participating in the regulation of the energetic functioning of the human organism. This is the principle of "grounding" developed by Lowen (1958). However, before the baby meets the ground on which he will stand and to which he will be connected, it is in the body of his mother that he will initially ground.

The energetic-sensory links manifest through affects of vitality. It was Lowen's fundamental theoretical and methodological contribution during the 20th century. It focuses on motility of the Self, energetic circulation and sensory awareness. The work on breathing holds an important place in this contribution.

The sensorimotor links, as was demonstrated by Piaget, manifest through the elaboration of sensorimotor schemes. Many "bioenergetic exercises" proposed by Lowen involve the elaboration of sensorimotor schemes that facilitate self-assertion through regulated and coordinated action.

The emotion-motor function links manifest through postural and behavioural patterns as Reich and Wallon have demonstrated during the same period of time, Reich in relation with the adult and Wallon in relation with the child. Lowen has developed other "bioenergetic exercises" that facilitate the expressiveness of the Self, particularly through the use of movement and emotional expression.

The emotion-representation or affect-representation links, theorized by Freud, manifest through cognitive representations (close to perception) and through fantastical representations (by-products of imagination). Those representations coexist, consciously or unconsciously, and constitute the contents of the mind. They are the subject of verbal analytical process.

These links between the various functions of the Self are conducive to the *integration of the Self*.

Motility and integration of the Self are being expressed at three levels:
➤ at the level of adaptive motility
➤ at the level of sexual motility
➤ at the level of affective attachment motility.

Starting at 2 years of age, the Ego progressively and essentially will have to co-integrate and co-regulate the adaptive, sexual and attachment motilities.

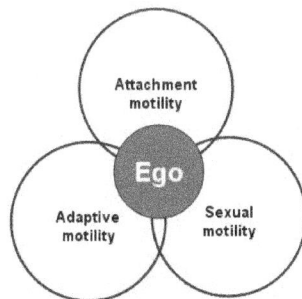

Attachment motility

Ego

Adaptive motility

Sexual motility

The function of the Ego

Paradigm II: Adaptive Motility and its Patterns

Throughout life, the Self is constantly obliged to adapt to external reality and to its modifications. In order to accomplish this, it counts on its life preservation instincts, as Freud, and later Lowen, have emphasized. Those instincts become the adaptive motility of the Self as it engages the environment on various levels: domestic *(Note of Translator: in the sense of "family")*, cultural, ecological.

The function of adaptive motility is to maintain the Self in a state of homeostatic vitality (a vitality that is energetically regulated) and in a state of perceptive consciousness (of itself and of the environment). It progressively organizes itself into adaptive patterns:

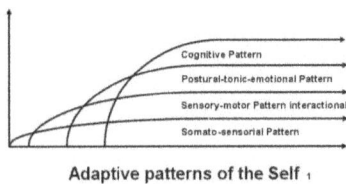

Adaptive patterns of the Self ↑

Somatosensory patterns organize and regulate the motility of the Self: sleep/awakeness, activation/deactivation, pleasure/pain, activity/passivity, expression/inhibition patterns, as well as multiple other configurations of vital expression. They are essentially coded in procedural memory but can be retrieved within the therapeutic context when bodily processes are emphasized, like during a piece of work on breathing or on sensory awakening. *Those patterns ensure permanent regulation of the vital existence of the Self.*

Sensorimotor patterns are built on the usual sensorimotor schemes and they organize the motility of the Selfʿ. Very early on, they are permeated with affect and according to Bowlby's expression (1969, 1973, 1980), they become "Internal Operative Models" (IOM) that organize attachment and interaction behaviours. Those IOM are encoded in procedural and episodic memories and are apt to be retrieved in therapeutic contexts that facilitate their evocation. The more presymbolical the IOM, the closer a context to the initial coding context will be needed in order for it to be recalled, which supposes a sensory, affective and motor activation. *Internal Operative Models ensure a regulated permanence of the interaction.*

Tonic-emotional postural patterns are built out of expressive interpersonal interactions and they organize the expression of the Self. For Wallon (1934), they have a socializing value: they communicate the affective experiences of the Self to the environment. For Reich (1933), they have a biological function:

they express pleasure/displeasure of an instinctual/sexual nature. Finally, for Ainsworth (1978), they support a behavioural function that manifests itself by secure/insecure „attachment patterns". In all cases, *those tonic-emotional patterns play the role of invariant affective expression of the Self.*

Cognitive patterns are built from perceptual images of self and of the surrounding world, both physical and human. They suppose mind processes and affective processes that facilitate adaptation to the environment. *They play the role of semiotic invariants (through images and words) within the Self.*

Those various patterns are adaptive because they continually activate motility, motor function, expressiveness and thought in a regulated, homeostatic way, nourishing what Damasio calls "The feeling of what happens" (1999).

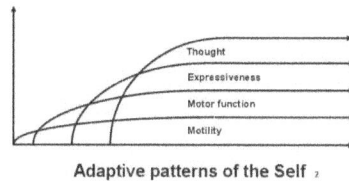

Thought
Expressiveness
Motor function
Motility

Adaptive patterns of the Self 2

Paradigm III: Sexual Motility and its Patterns

We are used to a model based on sexuality in Bioenergetic Analysis and I will be brief regarding this. On this matter, Lowen (1958, 1965, 1968, 1975, 1985, 1989, 1990, 2004) was Freud's (1905), then Reich's (1933, 1940) heir. We usually describe sexual motility in terms of oral, anal, phallic and genital impulses, first infantile, then adult genital drives.

Following Reich's footsteps, Lowen has demonstrated how each type of primitive drive is operating on a body level: their energetic dynamics in a particular part of the body that turns it into an „erogenous zone".

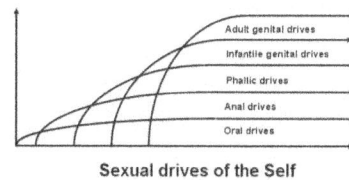

Adult genital drives
Infantile genital drives
Phallic drives
Anal drives
Oral drives

Sexual drives of the Self

It may be useful to mention that in a child, the activation of erogenous zones is closely related to mother-child interactions, hence to a mutual attachment relationship. A lack of or an excess of erogenization of the bodily self of the child has direct consequences on the organization of its sexuality, both present and future. A lack of erogenization (erogenic body sensations) can lead to erotic compulsion (sexual compulsion) as if it could bring erogenic sensations and fulfill that need.

From this point of view, *the experience of attachment (conflictive/traumatogenic attachment) during childhood determines adult sexual patterns.* Conversely, the therapeutic experience of attachment by building a more secure Self can have a direct impact on the transformation of adult sexual patterns.

Paradigm IV: Attachment Motility and its Patterns

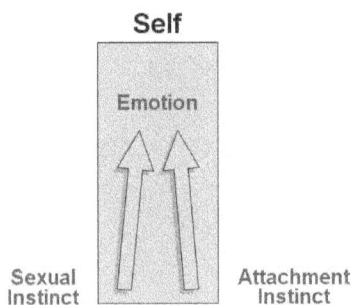

Self

Emotion

Sexual Instinct

Attachment Instinct

Following Freud and Reich, Lowen in 1958 places sexual instinct and sexuality at the core of bioenergetics' practice. At approximately the same time, Bowlby (1969) formulates the attachment theory.

Emotional expression then takes on two possible meanings for the child: either it is a signal of sexual pleasure/displeasure (Lowen), or it is a safety/distress signal (Bowlby).

Contemporary Bioenergetic analysis has gained by trying to integrate attachment theory as it acknowledged that *instinct of attachment exists at the beginning of life and is a structuring force as present and active as sexual instinct.*

The second half of the 20th century opened a large field of research that saw theoretical elaboration regarding attachment and interactive bonds so essential to the construction of the Self. If D. W. Winnicott and M. Malher were precursors, let us mention as well the first theoreticians of attachment theory: Bowlby, Ainsworth, Main, as well as the work of Wolf, Emde, Anders, Sander, Cassidy, Stern and others. They all contributed to the following demonstration: the Self, as a subjective identity-in-development, cannot be built without bonding and that bonding is the work of both partners, by their *mutual attachment* and their *interactivity*. I believe that this is true for the elaboration of the bonds between mother and baby, I equally think that it is true for the construction of the bonds between therapist and patient.

ATTACHMENT AND INTERACTIVE BONDS

The attachment and interactive bonds can be found in four types that gradually emerge from the encounter with the care-giver, generally the mother.

The existential bond participates in the emergence of the existential core of the Self, in the construction and afterwards in the secure reproduction of its somatosensory invariants. It is affirmed in the way baby and mother first look at each other, and is confirmed in their subsequent interactions that contain the organic excitation of the child, that shape his vitality and needs for contact. *The existential bond promotes and validates the phenomenological base of the living-being-that-exists* ("l'être-là-vivant") *throughout life.*

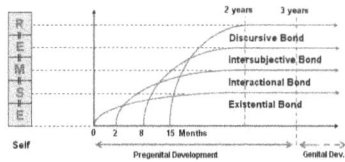

The Self and its bonds of attachment & interaction

The interactional bond participates in the emergence of the sensorimotor invariants that become the sensorimotor Internal Operational Models (IOM). Those models are initially activated by the needs for attachment and the needs for the exploration of the environment. The regulation of committed actions is related to the stimulation or the inhibition of sensorimotor IOM, according to adaptive needs. *The interactional bond ensures trusting reproduction of sensorimotor Internal Operational Models.*

The intersubjective bond facilitates the emergence of personal subjective states, and helps to make conscious that they are different from subjective states of another person. It is based in the capacity for attunment. *The intersubjective bond promotes the possibility to express and share its own subjective states with others.*

The discursive bond participates in the emergence of the capacity to reflect upon oneself, upon the relationship to one's internal and external world, as well as their objectivation. It is based on a capacity for shared meanings from a system of verbal communication. *The discursive bond promotes a coherent continuity between what is being experienced and what is being thought.*

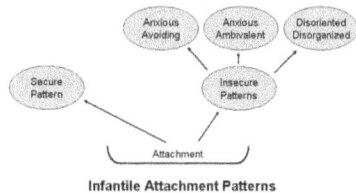

Infantile Attachment Patterns

When these bonds of attachment do not fulfil their organizing and regulating function, the child experiences anxiety. Ainsworth (1978), Main and Solomon (1988) show that he attempts to protect himself against anxiety by adopting three main types of attachment strategies: he can become *"anxious-avoiding"*, *"anxious-ambivalent"* or *"disorganized-disorientated"*.

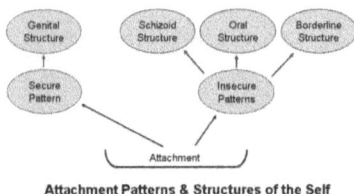

Attachment Patterns & Structures of the Self

We can establish bridges between these attachment strategies and our bioenergetic structures of personality: between the "detached" adult and the "schizoïd structure", between the "preoccupied" adult and the *"oral structure"*, between the "disorganized-disoriented" adult and the *"borderline personality"*.

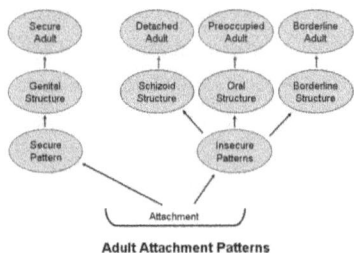

Adult Attachment Patterns

If the child or the adolescent does not have the possibility to evolve and build a pattern that is more secure, he then retains his infantile pattern. He becomes an adult that is *"detached"*, an adult that is *"preoccupied"*, or an adult that is *"disorganized-disoriented"*.

Those conceptual links enable us to clarify during the therapeutic process:

1) the origin of prevailing pathology (conflict, deficit or trauma),
2) the type of transferential attachment the patient actualizes, as well as the counter-transferential responses of the therapist.

PSYCHOPATHOLOGY OF ATTACHMENT

Relationships between psychopathology and bond of attachment need to be specified:

1) Attachment theory highlights the fact that the etiology of pregenital structures is not of a sexual nature but more of a deficit or traumatic nature.
2) The behavioural response to the deficit and the trauma brings into play a defensive organization that involves chronic muscular tensions. But if

the bodily tensions that originate from the deficit and the trauma, and the bodily tensions that originate from sexual conflict are intermingled and sometimes merge, their function is not identical. They will be expressed through transference in a significantly different ways.

3) Sexual problems that derive from developmental trauma are the expression of a traumatic attachment pattern and not of a sexual conflict. If the purpose of *character analysis* is to dissolve defensive reactions against sexual anxiety, the purpose of trauma therapy is *to renegotiate functional activity, integrative links and bonds of attachment* with the human environment that exists in the present.

NEUROBIOLOGY OF THE ATTACHMENT

Psychopathology of the bond of attachment is supported today by the investigations in neuroscience. Let me just give some examples:

Beaurepère (2003) shows that when an infant has been mistreated and sees his perpetrator, his right hemisphere goes into survival mode. If this situation is repeated, it is registered into implicit memory, it shapes an emotional habit and determines a style of attachment. He then barely needs to see this threatening attachment figure to produce stress hormones. In the long run, this repeated hormonal production will modify the somatic development: the volume of the hippocampus will decrease and there will be an increase of the volume in the temporal gyrus.

Evrard (1999) shows that the limbic circuit dies out when a little child cannot renew substitutive bonds of attachment when he loses his primary attachment figure. The absence of stimulations explains cerebral atrophy, the atrophy of the neurons that play an important role in the circuits of the memory and the acquisition of the emotional aptitude, in the hippocampus. Except in extreme cases, this process is reversible.

After the death of the Rumanian dictator Ceausescu, Ionescu (Ionescu et al.,

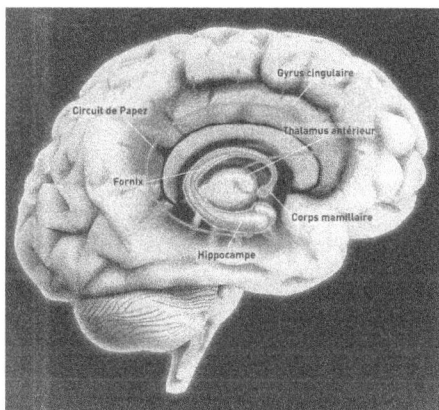

2001) wrote a report where he demonstrates that, in some forty institutions, children that were abandoned and deprived of attachment were found to be suffering from serious biological, emotional and behavioural disorders that are irreversible.

However, for the adult, disappearance of a loved one can cause a traumatic wound as serious as that of the infant who loses his mother. Parkes (Parkes et al, 1993), who has studied the biology of mourning, demonstrates that when an adult is attached to his/her partner in an anxious-insecure way, in the months that follow the loss of the partner, a peak of cardiac disease, pulmonary diseases, cancers, diabetes and mental confusion can be observed.

CLINICAL CONCLUSIONS

We are shown that attachment traumas are at the origin of specific pathologies that can deeply affect the Self, its construction, its bonds and its motility. *If conflict has functional consequences, trauma has functional and structural consequences.* We have to affirm and promote the existence of two different methodologies in bioenergetic analysis:

1) The methodology that consists in working with conflicts using character analysis;
2) The methodology that consists in working with traumas, which is quite different. Several of our bioenergetic colleagues have contributed to the development of the latter: Robert Lewis, Maryanna Heckberg, Helen Resneck-Sannes, Michael Maley, David Finlay, David Berceli as well as others.

Paradigm V: A Methodological Model for Trauma

In addition to the model of character analysis reserved for conflict issues, we now have models that help us understand and therapeutic practices that help us deal with issues related to trauma.

THERAPEUTIC MODELS RELATED TO TRAUMA

With his "cephalic shock" concept, Bob Lewis proposes a comprehensive model for developmental trauma (1976, 1984, 1986, 1998) which I will briefly summarize. This type of trauma originates in a non-empathic and dissonant holding and handling of the baby on the mother's part. The cumulative effect of repeated experiences of shock constitutes a traumatic experience:

➤ the infant develops strong muscular tensions in the nape of the neck, at the base of cranium: the perception of the head becomes dissociated from the perception of the body;

➤ by having to compensate for an inadequate mother, the infant *prematurely* holds his head up, thus prematurely developing a state of vigilance and an anticipatory perception. He *prematurely* develops his mental activity.

Thus the Self grows from a mental core that is dissociated from sensory and emotional experiences. There is a Self, located in the mind, in the thinking self, dissociated from the bodily Self. Such a child grows into an adult that lives in his head and by his head, in the literal as well as in the figurative sense.

The therapeutic process aims at re-establishing a secure therapeutic attachment relationship, allowing the patient to relax his head as well as the nape of his neck, which is dissociated from his body, so that he can work through his primitive anxieties in order be freed from them and to build a secure Self.

Maryanna Eckberg (1999), a bioenergetic therapist who has worked with political prisoners that were tortured, described her own methodology of traumatic shock treatment, inspired from Peter Levine's approach. Levine (1997) has proposed a general model with regards to trauma. He describes three types of defensive reactions in the face of a traumatic aggression: 1) attempt to fight against the aggressor (*fight*), 2) attempt to flee from the aggressor (*flight*), 3) faced with the failure, the organism freezes.

In this last case, the intense energy produced by the danger at the somatic level can neither be discharged nor metabolized. A breach has been opened in the envelope of the Self and functions like a "traumatic vortex": it attracts all the energies of the Self that are being is engulfed by this vortex. The usual somatosensorial patterns do not function any more, the feelings and perceptions do not acquire meaning any more. One is then confronted with bodily terror and the unthinkable at the psychic level.

Levine makes the assumption that a "healing counter-vortex", coming from an opposite direction, can be developed that could counterbalance the traumatic vortex allowing those people to experience a resilient co-integration.

In an article published in 2003, Bob Lewis has discussed Peter Levine's approach. He considers that this model is not complete enough to help us understand and treat developmental traumas because Levine does not integrate the lessons from attachment theory in his method.

Berceli (2003), a bioenergetic therapist, has developed a large group approach, based on his experience with populations that have been traumatized by wars, massacres, rapes, attacks, during NGO missions he was part of. He focuses his work on accessing tremors in body, a natural somatic reaction that enables the body to release enormous quantities of energy that have been generated by a traumatic event.

BODY APPROACH TO TRAUMA: A SPECIFIC METHODOLOGY

All the authors insist on 3 aspects: 1) the excessive quantity of energy mobilized by the traumatogenic situation could not be discharged and metabolized, 2) usual somatosensorial and tonic-emotional patterns do not function any longer, 3) representations of the traumatogenic situation cannot be expressed.

The methodology that is being used is quasi diametrically opposed to that of character analysis:

1) Regarding regulation *"titrage"* as opposed to catharsis:
    Titration, a concept that has been borrowed from chemistry, means meticulous regulation of the quantity of discharge energy at every moment, in order to control the return of traumatogenic experience, and in order not to replace a renegotiation of the traumatic experience by a traumatic cathartic replay.

2) Regarding a "window of tolerance" as opposed to maximum intensity:
    Seigel (1999) defines a window of tolerance that facilitates sensory awakening by allowing the return of sensory information (paralysis, feelings of numbness, rigidity, hyper-agitation, irritability, turbidity of wakefulness/sleep), in a modulated way, without waking up terror associated with the traumatic experience.

3) Regarding "micro-movements" as opposed to full and intense movements:
    Slow work allows a person to become aware, to explore, to disentangle issues, to recognize, to integrate, associate. The slowness of the work facilitates the analysis of each feeling, image or affect. This work makes it possible to leave

the frozen response, of frozenness of the organism's underlying structures, to gradually get involved again in defensive and orienting responses.

4) Regarding containment as opposed to "letting go":
The containing function of the therapist is essential because the patient's capacities to contain his/her feelings, to think and to act were exceeded during the traumatic experience. The aim of the work is to reconstitute a membrane that is at the same time tonic and flexible, that will be experienced as a containing and protective boundary for oneself. It goes beyond that and becomes a kind of psychic boundary apt to contain perceptions, images and representations.

5) Regarding re-initialization of defenses as opposed to releasing defenses:
The aim is to help the patient re-mobilize reactions that were repressed at the time the traumatogenic situation happened, to reconnect with the defensive and orientation responses that could not be expressed at the time, and to enable those reactions to surface.

This methodology to work on trauma is now seen as an essential therapeutic tool today:

1) in response to developpemental traumas that are forever increasing. They originate in the sociocultural evolution: mothers involved in a professional activity, the atmosphere in the family that is defined by poverty, unemployment and anxiety, urban violence, the uprootedness, isolation, etc...

2) in response to factual traumas that are on the rise, due to delinquency, violence, rapes, attacks, etc...

Finally, character analysis turns out to be relevant to treat genital conflicts as well as for regressions to pregenital positions that are triggered by conflicts generated by the Ego and the Superego, while psychotherapy of traumatic shock turns out to be relevant for the treatment of developmental traumas and the structural then functional distortions that they generate.

Paradigm VI: A Clinical Model for the Therapeutic Intervention: The Intersubjective Relation

INTERSUBJECTIVE ATTUNMENT

In 1985, Stern highlighted the concept of "attunement" in the relationship between mother and child. This attunement regulates the subjective states of the child and allows him to understand that his mother has a "spirit" different from his.

Fonagy (1994, 2000) has operationalized this intersubjective dimension in the therapeutic field. It is the therapist's Self, with its containing, feeling, thinking qualities as well as its capacity to express subjectively that is therapeutic, which the patient internalizes. The empathic therapist feels and imagines the inner states of his patient and he reflects it back to him through nonverbal as well as verbal answers. By "meeting himself in the other" the patient develops his capacities to feel, to contain and to elaborate his own subjective states. Experiencing that he is felt and thought by the other, one feels and thinks by himself.

I remember my first session with *Rafaël*: he is seated in front of me, he looks at me without seeing me, immobile, frozen, hardly breathing, terrified, I guess. I look at him quietly, affectionately. I ask him what is going on for him, but he does not hear me, or he cannot answer me. At the end of a long moment of silence, I say to him with kindness, but also with sadness: "I feel lonely … And you?" He looks at me, amazed, quiet, with some tears in his eyes. Then he says to me in a sad voice: "So do I …" He will reveal to me much later that he felt at the time that I was human, that I had access to feelings of loneliness, and that I could understand him. For sure, that feeling was not strange, my inner child had kept a memory which had found a companion in *Rafaël* and had signalled it to him.

SOMATOSENSORIAL EMPATHY

Schore (2001) highlights earlier somatosensorial attunements. By cerebral imagery, he shows that somatosensorial and emotional regulation of the child by his mother is organized from a body communication system recorded in a direct and unconscious interaction right brain – right brain.

Schore extends this discovery to the therapist – patient relationship, organized around the somatosensorial signals emitted by the patient, signals which the empathic therapist interprets from his own somatosensorial system, and to which he answers by attuned interventions.

I remember, in a hospital context, a schizophrenic young woman who held me by the hands, who was experiencing unthinkable anguish because she could not perceive where my hands "began" and where hers "finished". She was oscillating between terror of contact and irrepressible need for contact. Her psychotic anguish was founded on the absence of somatosensorial patterns giving her the clear sensation of a separate physical existence (Tonella et al., 1989; Tonella, 2006).

All the preverbal structures have problems of empathy. On the neurological level, Green (2004) found that they expressed a deficit in the amygdala activation. We, therapists, are amygdala activators. Because we have empathy, we invite our patients into a world of shared humanity.

Neurology of empathy

Empathy is more than a clinical concept, it is a neurological reality.

In 1996, Gallese, Fadiga, Fogassi, Rizzolati highlighted the existence of "mirror neurons" in the brain, that are in charge of the empathy. The therapist's occipital area, the part that processes images, sends the information that has been perceived to the fronto-temporal cortex, another part that prepares for action, thus alerting mirror neurons. The therapist, simply by perceiving and feeling without acting, can assess the emotional and subjective state of his patient.

In this brain imagery graphical, the black dotted line shows the activated neurons in the experiencing person (the patient); white dotted line shows the activated neurons in the person (the therapist) in relation-ship/observing the first one having the experience. One can observe that the same areas are activated within the limbic system (the straight black line) of both patient and therapist. The therapist's mirror neurons (the activated white dotted area) allow him to "rebuild" and feel the experience of the patient.

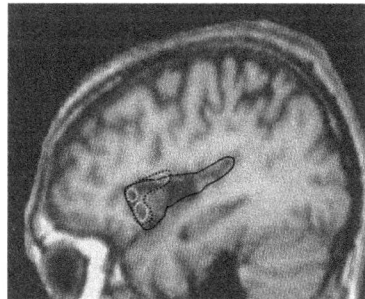

This year, Rizzolati, Fogassi, Gallese (2007) have shown that mirror neurons are missing among autistic patients. This has initiated a new therapeutic approach based on mutual imitation between the autistic patient and the psychotherapist, imitation underlying the development of the capacity for empathy.

NEUROLOGY OF TRANSFERENCE – COUNTERTRANSFERENCE

However, how do we explain that we do not respond systematically by action when our mirror neurons inform us of a state of distress or suffering in the patient? Grézes (1998) shows us that, although the temporo-frontal area needs to be activated in order to act, the prefrontal area responsible for inhibition of action is also activated. This double message activates a left ascending frontal cortical area responsible for the language. The answer of the therapist can then be formulated in words. We have here a first neurological draft of transference/counter-transference. Therapists could learn to dis-inhibit their body responses, whereas others could learn how to contain their impulses and transform them into verbal language.

THERAPEUTIC PROCESS AND RESILIENCE

Evrard, Marret, Gressens (1997) show that the fronto-limbic circuits are involved in the patterning of "sensitivity" since early infancy but they can be improved later on, prompting biological markers of stress to evolve (for example rate of serotonin transported by the 5-HTT Long versus 5-HTT Short proteins). This evolution rests on the possibility of rebuilding secure and trustful attachments. Psychotherapy must integrate this parameter in its setting, offering to the patient the occasion to reconnect with secure and decontextualisable therapeutic attachment.

CRITERIA OF COMPETENCE OF A THERAPIST

Ainsworth (1978, 1979) has described the criteria of competence for the mother so that she (the mother) can offer her child a secure attachment that enables him to develop a secure Self. It seems that these same criteria apply to a therapist who can help a patient develop a secure Self. This is confirmed by current research in the neurobiology of attachment. Let me remind you of these criteria:

1) the *development of trust in oneself* requires three criteria of competence on the part of the therapist: 1 – a therapist attached to his patient in a non anxious way; 2 – a therapist who is available to his signals; 3 – a therapist who responds to him in an adequate way;

2) the *development of self-confidence* supposes: 1 – a therapist who allows himself to be used by his patient when he tries to recreate something he has just discovered so as to help him succeed, 2 – a therapist-patient dyad in which the same causes bring the same consequences so that constancy and permanence become organizing factors in the interaction;

3) the *development of self-esteem* demands that the therapist confirms to his patient that his new capacities for action, expression, attachment and interaction have value. It facilitates reproductive assimilation.

The adult who suffers from attachment disorders harbours a little child who is still waiting for someone who can surrender to him so that he can regain confidence in his own existence and value. To possess and be possessed, this is the name of the game for children who need to develop the deep-seated belief that they are loved and that they are capable of love. It is what gives all its meaning to the phrase "To hold someone tight" in psychotherapy. The imprescriptible needs originate, after all, from the time when, as Winnicott says: "Love can be shown only in terms of caring for the body". It is, I believe, this experience that many patients are waiting for, secretly.

Many among us have already stressed the importance of intersubjective bonds: R. Lewis, 1976, 1986, 1998; R. Hilton, 1988/89; D. Campbell, 1991, 1995; M. Eckberg, 1999; D. Finlay, 1999, 2001; V. Heinrich, 1999; G. Tonella, 2000; H. Resneck-Sannes, 2002; M. Doess, 2004.

Finally, here are the therapeutic functions that enable the Self to become sufficiently secure:

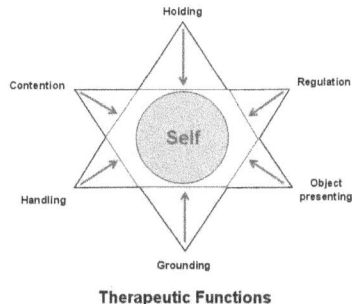

Therapeutic Functions

Paradigm VII: A Comprehensive Clinical Model

Let's see if we can now combine those various paradigms and their models, which we have just presented, in order to have a global vision of the theory and practice of Bioenergetic Analysis.

GLOBAL THEORETICAL MODEL

This model concerns the dynamics of the Self that is:
➤ oriented towards adaptation because of adaptive motility
➤ oriented towards interpersonal relationship because of attachment motility
➤ oriented towards sexuality (or the sublimation of it) because of sexual motility

Each of these activities of the Self gets organized at the very beginning of life into structuring and permanent patterns that are apt to evolve depending on life circumstances including psychotherapy.

DEVELOPMENTAL MODEL

The development of the Self, in its adaptations, in its sexuality and in its attachments can be described according to those four phases:

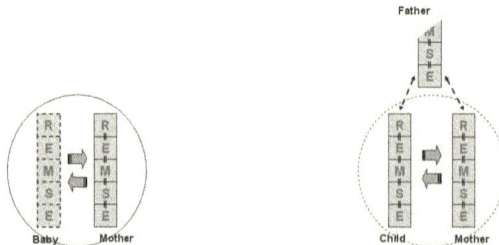

1) Oral phase of symbiotic attachment

2) Intermediate phase of individuated attachment

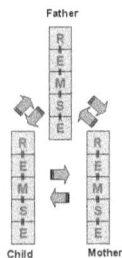

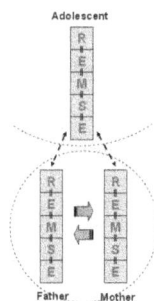

3) Genital infantile stage of reciprocal attachment

4) Adolescent stage of independent attachment

METHODOLOGICAL MODEL

The advantage of this model may lie in its capacity to help formulate a therapeutic strategy that is specific to each patient:

Various methodologies for various issues

➤ by emphasizing attachment motility and the construction of a secure attachment relationship when the patient's insecure attachment pattern acts as a major resistance to any therapeutic intervention (distress, terror, paralysis);

➤ by emphasizing adaptive motility (energetic charge increase, movement, emotional capacity for expression) when the vitality of the Self is in deficit;

➤ by emphasizing sexual motility and the resolution of sexual conflicts when they inhibit vitality and the Self's capacity for expression;

➤ by emphasizing re-initialization of the patterns of the Self when trauma damage or destroy it.

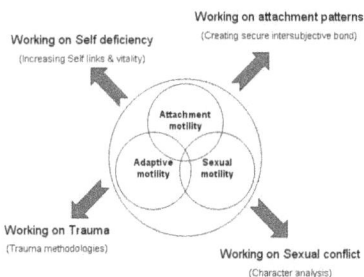

A therapeutic process obviously involves the total Self, but we can certainly argue that some people cannot work on themselves without having previously established a sufficiently secure therapeutic bond, which takes time. We can also argue that some sexual conflicts are nothing but the expression of an anxious attachment pattern and that the development of an enough-secure attachment during the therapeutic process is likely to resolve in part or totally the sexual issue.

RELATIONAL MODEL

Our relational model is marked by intersubjectivity, which means the inter-activity between therapist and patient. Therapeutic process is a co-creation between two persons. Various interactive communication systems contribute to it:

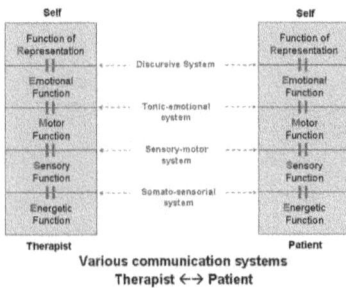

Various communication systems
Therapist ←→ Patient

Each of these systems facilitates specific dimensions like:

➤ interpersonal contact between two subjective Selves
➤ access to information of different nature (sensory, emotional, tonic, cognitive ...)
➤ activation of specific memories containing this information (procedural, episodic, semantic)
➤ regulation of the Self that refers at the same time to self-regulation and interpersonal regulation
➤ elaboration of these subjective states so that they gain meaning and enrich the Self.

The time has come for reconciling once and for all the individual experience and the interpersonal experience within the therapeutic process. We must nevertheless clarify that interpersonal experience does not mean "being in relationship" but means "being personally involved in a subjective relationship that is mutually shared and talked about".

Paradigm VIII: A Sociological Model Based on the Principle of "Shared Vitality"

Bioenergetics was a pioneer in initiating the work with vitality. Can it live up to that standard again? It can if we take into account the actual sociological evolution and the underlying demand of a "shared vitality" for a "shared world".

A new creativity is emerging, particularly in Brazil: new applications are already being developed by many among you:

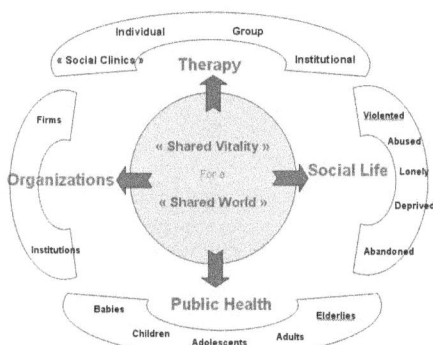

➤ *in public health* in relation to problems created by the sedentary way of life, the fast food culture, the traumas that disorient the Self: its functioning, its boundaries, its signals, generating somatic and relational malfunctioning;

➤ *at the micro-sociological level* for those forgotten minorities that face poverty, inequities, emotional separations that generate violence; places where vitality is not shared;

➤ *in business organizations* that are confronted with problems of communication, stress, loss of human contacts, robotization.

We, bioenergetic therapists, must become "readable and visible", seen as qualified professionals in all these fields. We suffer from the secrecy in which we maintain our reflections, our methodologies and our experience. We do not publish much; we are not on display in the bookstores, in professional journals, in regional or international Conferences.

Our approach is not taught in Universities, where most of the teachers ignore its existence. Our creativity is sometimes plundered or counterfeited. If we remain in the shade, we will disappear like those prehistoric animals that did not adapt to the changes in their environment and we will remain with the stereotyped image I was referring to, at the beginning of my talk:

"Bioenergetics is about shouting, crying, and kicking on the mattress". As a result, it becomes harder and harder to fill our training groups, at least in the United States and in Europe.

We are the bearers of relevant answers; contemporary scientific research validates our work. We are qualified to take up certain challenges today's world is confronting us with. It is difficult to take up challenges of this nature individually, on our own, but a whole community can succeed if it is alive, if it takes care of its *vitality* through its interactions, through its professional meetings, through its shared productions. This is exactly why we need to maintain these international meetings, beyond the barriers of language and distance.

Conclusion

Talking about the individual, Alexander Lowen used to speak so often of the importance of the heart. An organization also lives through its heart. I wish for all of us in the IIBA, the capacity to preserve and defend our values of *solidarity*, *fraternity* and *co-operation*. We are more than ever in need of these three institutional paradigms at a time when the world is being torn apart and faces "broken times".

References

OUR HERITAGE: BASIC PARADIGMS IN BIOENERGETIC ANALYSIS

Lowen A.: (1958), The language of the body, Grusse and Stratton, New York, 1977, trad. fr. Le Langage du Corps, Tchou, Paris.
Lowen A.: (1968), Expression of the self, Monograph, Institute for Bioenergetic Analysis, New York
Lowen A.: (1985), Narcissism, denial of the true self, Macmillan Publishing Company, New York, 1987,
trad. fr. Gagner à en mourir, une civilisation narcissique, Hommes et Groupes, Paris.
Lowen A.: (1965), Breathing, movement and feeling, Monograph, Institute for Bioenergetic Analysis, New York

Lowen A.: (1975), Bioenergetics, Coward, Mc Geogham Inc, New York, trad. Fr. (1976) La Bioénergie, Tchou, Paris

PARADIGM I – THE SELF, A PSYCHOSOMATIC CONTINUUM

Blake D.T., Byl N.N., Merzenich M.: (2002), Representation of the hand in the cerebral cortex, Behaviour Brain Research, 135, PP. 179–184
Jeannerod, M.: (2005), Le cerveau intime, Odile Jacob, Paris.
Kandel E.R.: (2001), The molecular biology of memory storage: a dialogue between genes and synapses, Science, 294, pp. 1030–1038
Freud, S.: (1887–1902), Aus den Anfängen der Psychoanalyse, 1954, trad. angl. The origins of Psychoanalysis, London, Imago, 1956, trad. fr. La naissance de la Psychanalyse, Paris, PUF
Freud S.: (1915a), Die Verdrängung, 1952, trad. fr.,Le Refoulement, in Métapsychologie, Paris, Galimard, pp. 67–90
Freud S.: (1915b), Das Unbewusste, 1952, trad. fr., L'Inconscient, in Métapsychologie, Paris, Gallimard, pp. 91–161
Freud S.: (1926), Hemmung, Symptom und Angst, 1965, Inhibition, Symptome et Angoisse, Paris, PUF
Reich W.: (1933), Charakteranalyse, 1949, Caracter Analysis, Wilhelm Reich infant Trust fund. 1971, L'Analyse Caractérielle, Payot, Paris.
Wallon H.: (1934), Les origines du caractère chez l'enfant, (1949) PUF, Paris
Piaget J.: (1936), La naissance de l'intelligence chez l'enfant, Delachaux et Niestlé, Paris
Lowen A.: (1958), The language of the body, Grusse and Stratton, New York, 1977, trad. fr. Le Langage du Corps, Tchou, Paris.
Lowen A.: (1968), Expression of the self, Monograph, Institute for Bioenergetic Analysis, New York
Lowen A.: (1985), Narcissism, denial of the true self, Macmillan Publishing Company, New York, 1987,
trad. fr. Gagner à en mourir, une civilisation narcissique, Hommes et Groupes, Paris.
Lowen A.: (1965), Breathing, movement and feeling, Monograph, Institute for Bioenergetic Analysis, New York
Lowen A.: (1975), Bioenergetics, Coward, Mc Geogham Inc, New York, trad. Fr. (1976) La Bioénergie, Tchou, Paris

PARADIGM II – ADAPTIVE MOTILITY AND ITS PATTERNS

Bowlby J.: (1969), Attachment and Loss, Vol. I, Attachment, The Tavistock Institute of Human Relations, 1978 trad. Fr., Attachement et Perte, Vol. I, Attachement, Paris, PUF
Bowlby J.: (1973), Attachment and Loss, Vol. II, Anxiety and Anger, The Hogarth Press and the Institute of Psychoanalysis, 1978 trad. Fr., Attachement et Perte, Vol. II, La Séparation, Angoisse et Colère, Paris, PUF
Bowlby J.: (1980), Attachment and Loss, Vol. III, Anxiety and Anger, The Hogarth Press and the Institute of Psychoanalysis, 1978 trad. Fr., Attachement et Perte, Vol. II, La Perte, Tristesse et Dépression, Paris, PUF
Wallon H.: (1934), Les origines du caractère chez l'enfant, (1949) PUF, Paris
Reich W.: (1933), Charakteranalyse, 1949, Character Analysis, Wilhelm Reich infant Trust fund. 1971, L'Analyse Caractérielle, Payot, Paris.
Ainsworth M.D.S., Blehar M.C., Waters E. et Walls S.: (1978), Patterns of attachment: a psychological study of the strange situation. Hillsdale, New Jersey, Erlbaum.

Damasio A.: (1999) The feeling of what happens, body and emotions in the making of consciousness, Harcourt Brace and Company, New York, trad. Fr. (1999) Le sentiment même de soi, corps, émotion, conscience, Odile Jacob, Paris.

PARADIGM III – SEXUAL MOTILITY AND ITS PATTERNS

Freud S.: (1905), Drei Abhandlungen zur sexualtheorie, 1962 trad. Fr., Trois Essais sur la Théorie de la Sexualité, Paris Gallimard

Reich W.: (1933), Charakteranalyse, 1949, Caracter Analysis, Wilhelm Reich infant Trust fund. 1971, L'Analyse Caractérielle, Payot, Paris.

Reich W.: (1940) The function of the orgasm, Orgone Institute Press, New York, (1952) trad. Fr. La function de l'orgasme, L'Arche, Paris.

Lowen A.: (1958), The language of the body, Grusse and Stratton, New York, 1977, trad. fr. Le Langage du Corps, Tchou, Paris.

Lowen A.: (1965), Breathing, movement and feeling, Monograph, Institute for Bioenergetic Analysis, New York

Lowen A.: (1968), Expression of the self, Monograph, Institute for Bioenergetic Analysis, New York

Lowen A.: (1975), Bioenergetics, Coward, Mc Geogham Inc, New York, trad. Fr. (1976) La Bioénergie, Tchou, Paris

Lowen A.: (1985), Narcissism, denial of the true self, Macmillan Publishing Company, New York, 1987,

trad. fr. Gagner à en mourir, une civilisation narcissique, Hommes et Groupes, Paris.

Lowen A;: (1989), Présentation du séminaire sur "Grounding in sexuality and love", A. Lowen, F. Hladky

Lowen A.: (1990), The spirituality of the body, McMillan, New York, (1993) trad. Fr., La spiritualité du corps, Ed. Dangles, St-Jean-de-Brayes.

Lowen A.: (2004), Honouring the Body, Bioenergetic Press, Alachua, Florida.

PARADIGM IV – ATTACHMENT MOTILITY AND ITS PATTERNS

Lowen A.: (1958), The language of the body, Grusse and Stratton, New York, 1977, trad. fr. Le Langage du Corps, Tchou, Paris.

Bowlby J.: (1969), Attachment and Loss, Vol. I, Attachment, The Tavistock Institute of Human Relations, 1978 trad. Fr., Attachement et Perte, Vol. I, Attachement, Paris, PUF

Bowlby J.: (1973), Attachment and Loss, Vol. II, Anxiety and Anger, The Hogarth Press and the Institute of Psychoanalysis, 1978 trad. Fr., Attachement et Perte, Vol. II, La Séparation, Angoisse et Colère, Paris, PUF

Bowlby J.: (1980), Attachment and Loss, Vol. III, Anxiety and Anger, The Hogarth Press and the Institute of Psychoanalysis, 1978 trad. Fr., Attachement et Perte, Vol. II, La Perte, Tristesse et Dépression, Paris, PUF

Ainsworth M.D.S., Blehar M.C., Waters E. et Walls S.: (1978), Patterns of attachment: a psychological study of the strange situation. Hillsdale, New Jersey, Erlbaum.

Main M. et Solomon J.: (1988), Discovery of an insecure-disoriented attachment pattern, in T. B. Brazelton et N. W. Yogman (Eds.), Affective development in infancy, 95–124

Evrard P.: (1999), Stimulation et développement du système nerveux, in J. Cohen-Solal, B. Golse, Au début de la vie psychique. Le développement du petit enfant, Paris, Odile Jacob

Ionescu S., Jourdan-Ionescu C.: (2001), La résilience des enfants roumains abandonnés, institutionnalisés et infectés par le virus du sida, in Manciaux (dir.), La résilience. Résister et construire, Genève, Médecine et Hygiène

Beaurepère R. de: (2003), Aspects biologiques des états de stress post-traumatiques, in J6M Turin, N. Baumann, Stress, pathologies et immunité, Paris, Flammarion, Médecine-Sciences; PP.135–153

Parkes C. M., Weiss R. S.: (1993), Recovery from Bereavement, New Yok, Basic Books

PARADIGM V – A METHODOLOGICAL MODEL FOR TRAUMA

Lewis, R.: 1976, Infancy and the head: The psychosomatic basis of premature ego development, Energy and character, Vol. 7, n°3.

Lewis R.: (1984), Cephalic shock as a somatic link to the false self personality, Comprehensive Psychotherapy, 4, 1984, Trad. fr. 1996, Le choc céphalique, une réaction somatique sous-tendant le faux "self", Les Lieux du corps, n°3, Ed. Morisset, Paris, 39–55.

Lewis R.: (1986), Getting the head to really sit on one's shoulders: a first step in grounding the false self, The Clinical Journal for Bioenergetic Analysis, Vol.2, n°1, 56–77.

Lewis R.: (1998), The trauma of cephalic shock: clinical case study, The Clinical Journal for Bioenergetic Analysis, Vol.9, n°1, 1–18.

Eckberg M.: (1999), Treatment of shock trauma: a somatic perspective, Clinical Journal of the International Institute for Bioenergetic Analysis, 10 (1), pp. 73–96

Levine P.: (1997), Waking the tiger; healing trauma, Berkeley, CA: North Atlantic Books, trad. fr, 2004, Réveiller le tigre. Guérir le traumatisme, Socrate Ed. Promex.

Berceli D.: (2003), Trauma Releasing Exercices, AZ, TRAPS

Lewis R.: (2003), Human trauma, Energy and Character, vol.3, pp. 32–40

PARADIGM VI – A CLINICAL MODEL FOR THE THERAPEUTIC INTERVENTION: THE INTERSUBJECTIVE RELATION

Stern D.: (1985), The interpersonal world of the infant, Basic books, Inc., Publishers, New-York, 1989, Le monde interpersonnel du nourrisson, PUF, Paris.

Fonagy P.: (1994), Mental representation from an intergenerational cognitive science perspective, Infant Mental Health Journal, 15, 57–68.

Fonagy P., Steele M., Steele H., Kennedy R., Matton G., Target M,: (2000), Attachment, the refletive self, and borderlines states, in Goldberg S., Muir R., Keer J., Attachment theory, Social development and Clinical perspectives, London, the Analytic Press.

Schore N. A.: (2001), The effects of a secure attachment relationship on right brain development, affect regulation and infant health, Infant Mental Health Journal, 22, 7–66

Tonella G., Jacomini V., Girard F., Granier F., et Escande M.: (1989), L'émergence de la douleur/souffrance en psychothérapie corporelle à médiation corporelle chez le psychotique, Psychologie Médicale, Vol.21, n°6, 698–700.

Tonella G.: (2006), Körperpsychotherapie und psychose, in Marlock G., Weiss H. (Eds), Handbuch der körperpsychotherapie, Stuttgart, New York, Schattauer, 734–740.

Green M. J.: (2004), La persécution (ressentie): un évitement actif, Neuroscience Biobehaviour Revue, 28 (3), PP.333–342

Gallese V., Fadiga L., Fogassi L., Rizzolati G.: (1996), Action recognition in the premotor cortex, Brain, vol.119, n°2, pp. 593–609

Rizzolati G., Fogassi L., Gallese V.: (2007) Les neurones miroirs, Science, janvier 2007

Evrard P., Marret S., Gressens P.: (1997), Genetic and environnemental determinants of neocortical development: clinical applications, in A. M. Galaburda, Y. Christen, Normal and abnormal development of the cortex, Berlin, Ipsen Foundation, p. 165–178

Grézes J., Costes N., Decety J.: (1998), Top-down effect of strategiy of the perception of human biological motion: a PET investigation, Cognitive Neuropsychology, 15, pp. 553–582

Ainsworth M. D. S., Blehar M. C., Waters E. et Walls S.: (1978), Patterns of attachment: a psychological study of the strange situation. Hillsdale, New Jersey, Erlbaum.

Ainsworth M. D. S.: (1979), Infant-mother attachment, American psychologist, oct.1979, Vol 34, 10, pp. 932–937, (1986), trad. fr. l'attachement mère-enfant, in R. Zazzo (Ed.), La première année de la vie, Paris, PUF, 17–27.

Lewis, R.: (1976), Infancy and the head: The psychosomatic basis of premature ego development, Energy and caracter, Vol 7, n°3.

Lewis R.: (1986), Getting the head to really sit on one's shoulders: a first step in grounding the false self, The Clinical Journal for Bioenergetic Analysis, Vol.2, n°1, 56–77.

Lewis R.: (1998), The trauma of cephalic shock: clinical case study, The Clinical Journal for Bioenergetic Analysis, Vol.9, n°1, 1–18.

Hilton R.: (1988–89), Narcissism and the therapist's resistance to working with the body, The Clinical Journal for Bioenergetic Analysis, Vol.3, n°2, 45–74

Campbell D.: (1991), The word made flesh, The Clinical Journal for Bioenergetic Analysis, Vol.4, n°2, 57–63.

Campbell D.: (1995), It takes two to tango, The Clinical Journal for Bioenergetic Analysis, Vol.6, n°1, 9–15).

Eckberg M.: (1999), Treatment of shock trauma: a somatic perspective, Clinical Journal of the International Institute for Bioenergetic Analysis, 10 (1), pp. 73–96

Finlay D.: (1999), A relational approach to Bioenergetics, The Clinical Journal for Bioenergetic Analysis, Vol.10, n°2, 35–52.

Finlay D.: (2001), Notes on intimate connections, The Clinical Journal for Bioenergetic Analysis, Vol.12, n°1, 9–28.

Heinrich V.: (1999), Physical phenomena of countertransference: the therapist as a resonance body, The Clinical Journal for Bioenergetic Analysis, Vol.10, n°2, 19–31.

Tonella G.: (2000), The interactive self – Le self interactif, The Clinical Journal for Bioenergetic Analysis, Vol.11, n°2, 25–59.

Resneck-Sannes H.: (2002), Psychobiology of affects: implications for a somatic psychotherapy, The Clinical Journal for Bioenergetic Analysis, Vol.13, n°1, 111–122.

Doess, M.: (2004), Physical contact and construction of a therapeutic intersubjective bond, The Clinical Journal for Bioenergetic Analysis, Vol.14, n°1, pp. 01–18

About the author

Doctor in Clinical Psychology, Master in Psychophysiology, Psychotherapist, Co-Director of the Collège Français d'Analyse Bioénergétique, Member of the Faculty of the IIBA working with training groups in most of the European countries, Argentina, Brazil and Canada.

He taught psychology at the University of Toulouse (France) for 20 years.

He wrote "L'Analyse Bioénergétique" (Dalilo, Paris, 1994), "Analisis Bioenergetica" (Gaia, Madrid, 2000), chapters in "Handbuch der Körperpsychotherapie" (Stuttgart, Schattauer, 2006), in "Les Résiliences" (Erès, Toulouse, 2007), and around 40 articles in professional magazines.

Guy Tonella
Les Garrigues
31450 – ISSUS
FRANCE
guy.tonella@wanadoo.fr

Psychoanalyse der Lebensbewegungen. Zum körperlichen Geschehen in der psychoanalytischen Therapie – Ein Lehrbuch

Book Review by *Angela Klopstech*

German speaking thinkers and writers are excellent at compressing a complex concept that requires at least an entire paragraph in English into one (long) word. Metaphors like 'Zeitgeist' and 'Weltanschauung' are familiar to many therapists in the English speaking world who are philosophically, historically, or politically inclined, but how about the metaphor 'Lebensbewegungen'? In "Psychoanalyse der Lebensbewegungen", a recently published German reader, Peter Geißler and Günter Heisterkamp, chose this word creation as title for their edited collection of articles on bodily perpectives in psycho-analytic therapy.

It is a metaphor that, from a bioenergetic perspective, is intriguing and yet hard to translate. The best approximate translation seems to me "Psychoanaly-sis of Vitality" or "Psychoanalysis of Human Living Processes" which captures the authors' holistic inclinations to "view all utterances and expressions of the psyche, mental and bodily, as an integral part of an evolving whole" (p vii). It also captures to some degree their emphasis on the shaping and reshaping, and ever evolving nature of internal states and external expressions of the psyche. "Lebensbewegungen", which might literally be translated as "movements of/in/into/towards/for life", is an intriguing word construction because it has faint echoes of the Reichian principle of the pulsatory nature of all living processes. Intended by the authors or not, it seems appropriate for inclusion in the title of a book subtitled 'A primer of reflections on the bodily dimen-sion in psychoanalytic therapy'.

While we, bioenergeticists (my own word-creation, after all I was born German), are absorbing, redefining and integrating more and more of traditional and contemporary psychoanalytic concepts (articles in this issue and recent issues of 'Bioenergetic Analysis, the Clinical Journal of the IIBA' are testimony to this phenomenon), psychoanalysts, in turn, are doing the same with notions and concepts germane to body psychotherapy. This development is more advanced and professionally visible in the German/Austrian/Swiss axis than in the US. There, more publications are occurring in this arena by psychoanalysts and psychoanalysts turned analytical body psychotherapists. There is even a journal devoted to the theme "Psychoanalyse und Körper" (Psychoanalysis and the Body) with Geißler as editor.

These reaching out efforts from both sides have resulted in some overlap of conceptualizations and treatment approaches between bioenergetic analysis and body-oriented relational psychoanalysis, since both are psychodynamically based therapy schools, both employ and emphasize relational concepts, and both view bodily phenomena as essential to the enterprise. But there are also vast philosophical and treatment differences since the respective therapeutic frames remain quite apart from each other, and above all, the body is still at the heart of bioenergetic theory and practice while the relational aspect is at the heart of modern psychoanalysis. Being familiar with both, the overlap and the differences, can assist bioenergetic therapists in positioning themselves in the broader therapy world. And in this endeavor, this edited collection of articles can be helpful.

Starting out from the traditional notion that transference and counter-transference constitute the core of psychoanalytic treatment, Geißler and Heisterkamp arrive at a therapeutic setting called alternately analytical body psychotherapy or body-oriented analysis or body-based psychoanalysis (p vi, 301). This is a loosely defined "open setting" or "transitional space" that allows for and encourages a variety of interactions beyond the purely verbal. Heisterkamp states that "paying attention to and dealing with the bodily experience in the same measure as with the mental experience expands the realm of possibilities for the patient and brings childhood memories and present life situations into the present moment within the therapeutic encounter", and this results in "deepening the analytical process and expanding treatment possibilities" (p 300, 301). In this context of analytical body psychotherapy, the focus is on the bodily experience in the immediate interaction in the therapy dyad, the body 'in action' within the interaction, the body in the present moment and as the bearer of communication from within the patient and in between patient and therapist. This view of the body is similar to the view of the body in contemporary bioenergetic analysis with one crucial difference: in bioenergetic analysis the body is not only defined via its subjective experience but equally dealt with as a physical entity in and for itself.

An important feature of the book as a whole is the fact that all contributors elaborate on relevant notions and concepts that belong within the expanded frame and transitional space created by emphasizing the interactive and the bodily aspect in psychoanalytic therapy: dialogic interaction (Handlungsdialog), hypothesis-guided interaction (Inszenierung), enactment, implicit relational knowing (implizites Beziehungswissen), body-related micro practices (körperliche Mikropraktiken), self regulation, etc. These are notions and concepts that either were redefined in relational terms or entered psychoanalytic and psychotherapeutic writing in the last twenty years. In this context, most chapter authors straddle the divide between being analysts and body psychotherapists, and the editors themselves are both trained in psychoanalysis and bioenergetic analysis.

The reader begins with an introduction by the editors and a reflection on the theme as well as an overview of the various contributions by H.Müller-Braunschweig. There are then five parts to the book. The first deals with the foundational concepts of Analytical Body Psychotherapy, with contributions by J.Küchenhoff, U.Volz-Boers, S.Bettighofer, J.M.Scharff, P.Geißler and A. v.Arnim/P.Joraschky/H.Lausberg. Of particular interest here are the articles by Geißler and Bettighofer, because both give a detailed and profound overview of the professional field and terminology, the first with regard to developmental concepts, the latter with regard to transference/countertranference phenomena seen from an interactive perspective.

The second part focuses on general treatment aspects, with articles by G.Heisterkamp/P.Geißler, G.Worm, G.Poettgen-Havekost, T.Moser, G.Heisterkamp. Here Heisterkamp's article stands out because of the clinical relevance for everyday bioenergetic practice. He breaks the notion of interactive dyad/therapeutic encounter down into its nitty gritty details and components in order to take an in depth look at what is easily, often too breezily labeled as 'interaction' between therapist and patient. This is nicely dovetailed by Worm whose article provides an in depth look at resistance analysis in body-oriented analytical psychotherapy.

The third part deals with treatment aspects in a group setting, with contributions from R.Maaser, R.Heinzel and R.Ware. The articles in this section could be of interest to the reader because there is just so little literature on body psychotherapy in a group setting.

The fourth part looks at specific clinical application and specific disorders, with articles by D.Hoffmann-Axthelm, R.Ware, T.Reinert, M.Steiner-Fahrni and G.Downing. Hoffmann-Axthelm's article deserves particular mention because she elaborates on a set of treatment strategies that any bioenergetic therapist could easily integrate. George Downing may be familiar to US bioenergetic therapists since his original roots are in bioenergetic analysis and since he is a native English speaker with numerous publications in English. In this volume he writes about how to initiate therapy with difficult patients.

Last but not least, the fifth part looks to the future regarding a possible integration of analytical body psychotherapeutic concepts into postgraduate analytical training, by P.Geißler, G.Heisterkamp und T.Moser, and ends with a philosophical reflection by R.Kühn.

It was a smart move by the editors to focus on a mainly clinical and practical orientation for their reader; even the contributions attempting to break theoretical ground include clinical vignettes. This makes a voluminous (680 pages!), at times ponderous and repetitive book more readable and for extended stretches interesting. I certainly recommend it for those bioenergetic therapists in the German speaking world who want to familiarize themselves with recent developments in the psychoanalytic world close to their own professional home.

Review of *'Psychoanalyse der Lebensbewegungen': Zum körperlichen Geschehen in der psychoanalytischen Therapie – Ein Lehrbuch*; by Peter Geißler and Günter Heisterkamp (eds), 680 pages, Springer, Wien/New York, 2007

Dipl.-Psych Dr. Angela Klopstech
40–50 East Tenth Street, #1c
New York, NY 10003
Tel/Fax: 212–2603289
klopkoltuv@aol.com

Your Core Energy is Within Your Grasp

Bennett Shapiro

Summary

This paper, an abridgement of a 55-page paper, *Curling: Exercises and Notes,* highlights a new gentle approach to stimulating instinctual life-energy, helping restore natural energetic pulsation, and providing containment for building boundaries.

A soft curling and uncurling of the fingers and/or toes, in rhythm with the regular breathing pattern, brings up a mild, expansive, pleasurable energetic charge, which can then be augmented with simple body movements, eyes and words to help repossess repressed natural instincts. If stronger, more assertive energy is desired, the curl can be held tighter and longer.

This paper outlines six Curling exercises, useful both in the therapeutic setting and as self-help. The exercises can be done standing, sitting or lying down, and can be both relaxing and/or revitalizing. Some exercises can be done in bed, for helping to fall asleep, for example, or for an invigorating way to wake up.

Keywords: boundary, charge, contain, energetic, exercises

I Introduction

What are the Basic Motions and Rhythms of Curling?

First, gently start curling your fingers and toes in unison. (Finger-curling charges the *upper body* while toe-curling charges *the pelvis and legs*.) All motions, including the breathing, should be natural, gentle and unforced to allow a flow of pleasure in your body. Do not force the extension of fingers (Fig. 1) or toes (Fig. 2). There should only be a partial curling of your fingers, so that your fingernails do not touch the palms (Fig. 3); nor should the toes be curled too tightly (Fig. 4).

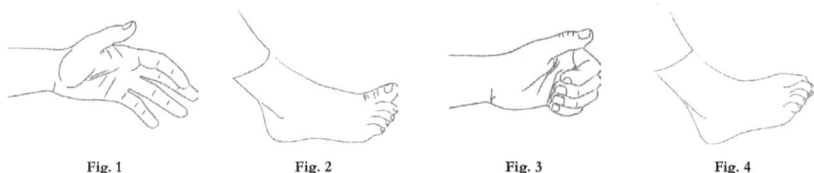

Fig. 1   Fig. 2   Fig. 3   Fig. 4

figure 1–4

Next, *inhale* as you extend the fingers and toes and *exhale* as you curl them. (This is the preferred pattern.) Once you have coordinated the breathing pattern with the extension and curling, you should stop. Remember, this is only an *orientation*, not an exercise.

Who Benefits from Curling Exercises?

➤ *New/vulnerable clients:* Curling exercises very gradually and gently enlarge the capacity for expansion/contraction, for increasing energetic charge/discharge, and for inducing revitalization/relaxation; they are therefore ideal as an introduction to energetic work for new or vulnerable clients and for frozen or traumatized clients.
➤ *Clients whose boundaries are too porous, too open:* As curling exercises

promote both energetic containment and ego control over instincts, impulses and feelings, they help build boundaries for those clients whose boundaries are too porous, too permeable, and who are too easily overwhelmed or who overwhelm others.

➤ *Inhibited clients:* Curling exercises can be used to loosen inhibited self-expression in the eyes, the voice and simple body movements, and to repossess instincts for reaching out to the world and obtaining satisfaction, fulfillment and pleasure.

➤ *Self-helping clients:* As curling exercises are simple and pleasurable, clients easily adapt them for daily self-help use; e.g., when lying in bed, sitting at home, or in the office.

➤ *Clients in recovery:* Curling exercises are being explored for recovery from medical operations, for disabled clients and for use by both in-patients and out-patients in a psychiatric hospital.

II The Components of a Curling Exercise

A. Physical Position

Physical positions can be standing, sitting, lying on the back, lying on the belly or lying on the side, as shown in Table 1, Section III. Positions have infant, child and adulthood associations – e.g., lying down may feel more vulnerable than standing.

B. Energetic Charging/Containing/Discharging

Charging: The mild charge generated by alternating between extension and curling can be greatly increased by verbalization of a developmental instinct (Component C), by self-expressive movements, eyes and voice and the use of boundary-building 'props', e.g., pillows (Component D). This greater charge/discharge can then lead to more relaxation and more *pleasure*.

Containing: Clients consciously generate all movements, expressions and verbalizations themselves, and the buildup of the charge is slow and gradual.

Therefore it is unlikely that the clients will feel overwhelmed, since the slow and deliberate pace is sufficient containment in and of itself.

Discharging: The vibrations, quivering or involuntary movements that occur during the exercises indicate that the body has become charged and is now discharging. In order to discharge excess energy, exercises should conclude with bending over and grounding into the feet and legs.

C. Verbalizing a Developmental Instinct

I use the term "developmental instinct" to mean an instinct that moves a human being, in relationship to others, to seek satisfaction, fulfillment and pleasure while remaining connected to herself. In many of us these instincts have been withdrawn inwardly as a result of primal injuries.

Following are some instincts important to clients, listed in developmental order:

➤ "I can go out to the world ... and come back to myself."
➤ "I can go out to the world ... gather in something (or someone) and keep them for me."
➤ "I can go out to the world, see you, sense you, and then come back to myself and sense what I'm feeling physically and emotionally from having connected with you."
➤ "I can go out to the world, be sexually attracted to you, reach out and enfold you in my arms."

The words "I can" means that the Adult (observing ego) can own the desire to repossess this instinct. "I can" avoids an "I will" or an "I should," which may not be the intent of the client.

Also, the mild expansive energetic charge stimulated by curling provides a measuring tool for exploring the deficits/traumas in a developmental instinct. First, the expansive flow is stimulated by extending/curling the fingers and toes in rhythm with natural breathing. Then a verbalization is introduced, e. g., "I can go out to the world... and I can come back to myself." Accompanying the verbalization of the instinct is an associated body movement of hands, arms, legs and eyes for going out to the world and different body movements for coming back to oneself.

The client then takes note of any change in their energetic flow and body sensations – e.g., is there more excitation in thinking "I can go out to the world" and making the associated movements? Or is there more excitation in thinking, "… and I can come back to myself," with its associated movements? Does "going out" feel more risky? Does "coming back" feel more secure, safer?

Clients experience this procedure as being very revealing in a gentle, kind way. For example, some clients weren't conscious they had a clear choice to be "in" or "out," that it's possible to alternate between the two, and some are surprised to discover that they'd rather be "in."

D. 'Accelerators' (Self-Expressive Movements, Eyes and the Voice)

Each accelerator involves alternating slowly and rhythmically between two *polarities*, e.g., eyes alternating between open and closed. The rhythm of each accelerator is superimposed upon those of inhalation/extension and exhalation/curling. 'Accelerators' can greatly increase Curling's mild energetic charge; therefore a new/vulnerable client can only contain the added excitement of two or three accelerators, whereas a therapist/advanced trainee can integrate many. Of new and particular note are accelerators involving the tongue, the back, the heart, and props for boundary-building.

1.   TONGUE

Letting the tongue hang out *limply* from the *corner* of the mouth (Fig. 5) stops the ability to make words and makes thinking more difficult. Hence it is ideal for clearing the mind for really relaxing. When coupled with a smile, eyes open with excitement and charged arms reaching forward, the tongue out the corner of the

figure 5

mouth, brings up the excited Natural Child (core energy) with all its heartfelt intensity toward life. This maneuver stimulates a lot of strong positive excitement that is normally suppressed. The strong charge then moves quickly to the periphery of the body and generates great overall body heat with very little muscular effort.

In addition, the tongue hanging out limply from the corner of the mouth deepens *all feelings*, e. g., expressions of anger or fear. Moreover, some clients find that once they have experienced their excited Natural Child (see Exercise B), their tongues will emerge spontaneously as they express deeper feelings. People concentrating on a manual task do likewise.

2.   BACK

In Curling, arching the back *longitudinally* will increase the aggressive (assertive) charge. This is done most easily by slightly pressing backward on the shoulders and buttocks on inhalation. Also, letting the head go backward on inhalation assists the arching; letting it come forward on exhalation accommodates relaxing the back.

All the above movements are naturally inherent in every inhalation and every exhalation. By deliberately exaggerating the arching and relaxing, the client begins to breathe gradually more spontaneously and deeply. And when coupled with expressing an emotional feeling, the effect on breathing can be surprisingly strong (e. g., see Exercise C).

figure 6

3.   HEART

To help encourage the heart to open, the back needs to arch *laterally* as well as longitudinally (see above). In Curling this is done on inhalation by extending charged arms, wrists and hands fully out to the sides and about a foot back (see Fig. 6). Then on exhalation, bring your arms forward and across your chest, curling both hands around the edges of a pillow (see Fig. 7). Also, letting the head go backwards on inhalation helps to open the throat (a gateway to the heart); letting the head come forward on exhalation provides protection for vulnerability in the throat and heart. A fully detailed exercise for opening the heart is described in Shapiro, B. (2007).

4.   PROPS FOR BOUNDARY-BUILDING

Props stimulate an expansive energetic charge by providing a boundary for excitation, as did the mother's body. Substitutes for the mother's body include pillows for the chest and between the legs, soft fabric under the arches and toes to curl into and for the palms to curl into (see Fig. 8).

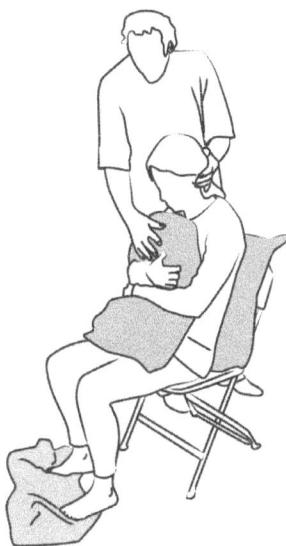

figure 7

5.   OTHER ACCELERATORS

Many other accelerators can be utilized, i.e., the eyes, the voice, the mouth and teeth, lips, jaw, arms, hands, legs and pelvis. In Exercises A to F, the uses of some of these more traditional accelerators are described in greater detail.

E.   Perceiving Pleasurable Sensations

The pleasurable sensations induced by Curling exercises include:
➤ Warmth or tingling or streaming

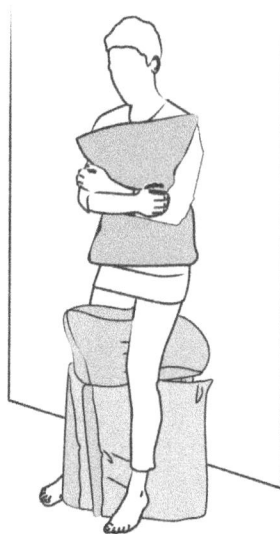

figure 8

➤ Perceiving energy flowing through a body part not previously a source
of pleasure, e.g., the feet
➤ Revitalization – a feeling of aliveness and wanting to be involved with life
➤ Letting down, relaxation

In Curling, pleasurable body sensations are more likely to arise because the
charge/discharge cycle occurs in conjunction with rhythmical movements,
e.g., inhale/exhale, extend/curl. (Rhythm is an important part of pleasure, as
Lowen, A. (1970) notes.

Also Curling exercises give clients an ideal opportunity to explore their
limits in perceiving pleasurable body sensations. The low level of charge/dis-
charge and the slow pace of the charge/discharge cycle, in rhythm with the
natural breathing pattern, help to lessen initial awkwardness/anxiety about
perceiving bodily pleasure. If an accelerator is added to an exercise, with
the subsequent addition of more excitation and another rhythm, the client's
boundary issues could become apparent to her as she finds herself struggling
to integrate the increased pleasure.

F. Strengthening Adult Functioning

The first task of strengthening Adult functioning is just to *locate* the Adult
and then get it more *present!* Fortunately, our Adult *can* be located and
strengthened simply by alternating between perceiving our outer world and
perceiving our inner world.

Curling exercises are ideal for alternating perception because with every
extension of our fingers and toes we are opening up to the world, and with
every curling of fingers and toes we go inward, back to ourself. Strengthening
our Adult in this way is analogous to strengthening the biceps by repeatedly
extending and bending the arm at the elbow.

The slow pace of Curling enables our Adult to stay present and make many
sequential deliberate decisions. Usually we act impulsively or too rigidly, either of which can easily overwhelm our Adult. In Curling, the basic motions
and rhythms are coupled with the verbalization of a developmental instinct
and the expressive gestures of the accelerators. This requires initial *control*
of the voluntary musculature, *coordination* of breathing together with the

curling, and *containment* of the resulting energetic flow. The slow, rhythmic and deliberate pace allows underlying *perception* of these capacities and of the energetic charge and resulting pleasure. All the above activities strengthen the Adult (observing ego) by exercising it.

III. Six Curling Exercises

Table 1 outlines the six exercises A through F. Exercise A is introductory. Exercises B and C are playful and light-hearted. Exercises D, E and F may initially require a therapist's help.

EXERCISE A	EXERCISE B
"I can open up ... and I can close down	*The Excited Natural Child Reaching Out*
• The introductory exercise; provides grounding through curling • Charges/discharges whole body while grounding • Introduces use of developmental instincts, accelerators, and perception of pleasure	• The quickest, easiest and most fun way to bring up the intense aliveness, excitement and warmth of core energy • Charges arms, wrists and hands for reaching out • Key accelerators: letting tongue hang out limply from the corner of the mouth, opening eyes wide and smiling

EXERCISE C	EXERCISE D
Laughing	*"I can go out to the world … and come back to myself"*

• The most enjoyable and spontaneous way to deepen breathing and for revitalization • Illustrates the power of the "body curl" to open the throat and chest and respiration • Limp tongue deepens the breathing cycle and revitalization even more	• Develops the ability to alternate between the polarities of being inside ourself or out in the world • Clarifies that we need to make conscious decisions whether to be "in" or "out" • By alternating between perception of inner and outer experiences, we discover what is fearsome and what safe

EXERCISE E	EXERCISE F
"I can open out … and gather in and keep for me"	*"I can feel fear … but I can hold myself together"*
• Mattress provides a boundary for, and supports and strengthens, the aggressive flow of energy in the back	• Provides a safe container for exploring fears that pull our energy 'up' and 'in' so that we cannot let down
• Arching back lengthwise further charges the aggressive component; arching it sideways opens chest and tender feelings	• Therapist's hand(s), mattress and wall provide a simultaneous boundary for front, back and feet
• Gathering in and keeping for oneself involves arms, legs and mouth (teeth)	• Curling in this position without a verbalization or exploration of fear lets you relax deeply and even sleep

Table 1: Curling Exercises

Exercise A: "I can open up … and I can close down" (standing)

This exercise introduces you to the basic rhythms and motions of Curling while leaning slightly against a wall and holding a pillow to your chest. The resulting energetic charge achieves some 'grounding,' especially if you bend over and hang down at the conclusion.

Equipment: a wall or closed door to lean against; a pillow; some soft fabric for feet.

1) To 'ground' through curling, lean against the wall/door, feet hip-width apart and heels at least 10 inches out from the wall to allow toe curling without losing your balance (Fig. 9). (If any leg-stress occurs, slightly bend and straighten your knees; never lock your knees!) Holding a pillow to your chest with crossed arms:
   - On *inhalation*: gently extend your wrists, fingers and toes; see Fig. 10.
   - On *exhalation*: gently curl your fingers around the pillow edges and your toes into the soft fabric (not shown in Fig. 9).

2) Once you have established the rhythm, relax your jaw, close your eyes and:
   - On *inhalation*, think, "I can open up;"
   - On *exhalation*, think, "… and I can close down."

3) When you feel you've had enough excitation and involuntary movement, stand up, bend over, let your fingertips touch the floor, and bend and straighten your knees slightly to allow vibratory movement in your legs; then come back to a standing position.

4) To incorporate arching and unarching your back, after repeating Steps 1 and 2:
   - On *inhalation*: gently extend your fingers/toes, arch the back by pressing shoulders and buttocks lightly against the wall; let your head fall back slightly.
   - On *exhalation*: gently curl fingers around the pillow edges and toes into the soft fabric; let your back relax and head come forward slightly.

Note: your back will slide slightly up the wall on inhalation and down the wall on exhalation.

5) Once you have established the rhythm of arching and unarching your back:
   - On *inhalation*, think, "I can open up" as you rise up slightly and extend fingers/toes;
   - On *exhalation*, think, "… and I can close down" as you slightly come down and curl fingers/toes.

6) Continue until you feel some vibrations or involuntary movement. If you wish to deepen your feeling of being able to "open up" and/or your feeling of being able to "close down:"

➤ On *inhalation*, open your eyes with excitement, reach softly with your lips (letting the lower jaw stay relaxed), smile and think about being able to open to the world;

➤ On *exhalation*, close your eyes and mouth and strongly bring your lower jaw forward in your determination to protect yourself by shutting out the world.

7) Option: To increase charge/discharge substantially, put pillows between your legs (see Fig. 8).

8) What are your emotional and bodily feelings about being able to "open up" and/or "close down" and being able to alternate between the two? If you are familiar with traditional 'grounding' techniques, how does 'grounding' through Curling compare?

9) To perceive pleasurable sensations in your body:

➤ Hold a pillow to your chest, arms crossed over the pillow, hands curling around the pillow edges, and close your eyes to focus on sensations in your body. Keep bending and straightening your knees very slightly.

➤ Leaning slightly against the wall to keep your balance:

➤ On *inhalation*, extend your fingers and toes and think, "I can feel my body;"

➤ On *exhalation*, think, "And I can feel its pleasure," or "I can feel ... and I can flow," or just "Feel ... flow."

You may need to moderate the intensity of the sensations in order not to lose perception of pleasure. An internal or external sigh of pleasure is helpful.

When you've had enough, open your eyes and come back to the world.

Exercise B: The Excited Natural Child Reaching Out (standing)

This exercise allows the energetic charge from grounded feet and vibrating legs to fully excite your Natural Child as it reaches, with all its heartfelt intensity, out to life. The exercise evokes a lot of fun, and feelings of great aliveness and body warmth when the core energy reaches the periphery.

Note: Read this exercise before beginning, to grasp the intent of the sequence of steps. Also review "Tongue," Component D (Accelerators).

Equipment: A wall (or closed door) to lean against.

1) 'Ground' your feet and legs: see Exercise A, Steps 1 to 4.
2) To charge your arms, wrists and hands, hold your hands in front of your chest and, strongly pressing the fingertips together (as in Fig. 11), turn the fingertips toward your chest until your arms begin to tremble. (Reaching out is sabotaged if your arms/hands are limp/flaccid.) Meanwhile continue to charge your legs.

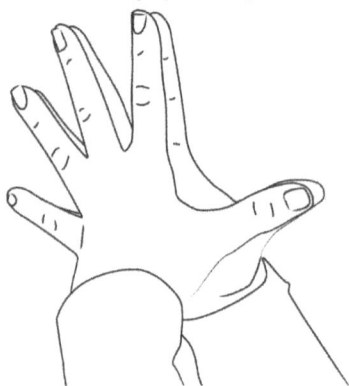

figure 11

3) Imagine you are a little toddler at a playground for children your age. You see a little friend of yours slowly coming toward you, with a big smile on his/her face, tongue hanging out the corner of his/her mouth and reaching out to you:

➤ Let your tongue hang *limply* out of the *corner* of your mouth, open your eyes with excitement, smile and make an "Egh–egh–egh" sound (or whatever sound comes naturally).

➤ Keep leaning against the wall for balance, so that you can reach with strong intent in Step 4.

4) Slightly bending your elbows and *rigidifying your arms, wrists, hands and fingers* so that they shake with tension:

➤ On *inhalation*, reach out to your little friend with *charged* (not limp) arms and hands. Smile with your tongue out and your eyes open with excitement. See Fig. 12.

➤ On *exhalation*, close your eyes and bend your elbows so that your arms retract slightly.

5) Press the balls of your feet against the floor to increase your excitation and send more vibratory movement

figure 12

up your body. As you keep reaching, your body may wish to involuntarily bounce up and down with all the excitement – just let it happen!

6) When you've had enough reaching out, bend over and sense the feelings in your legs, and your feet as they meet the floor. You may wish do some good-humored laughing about your experience as you are hanging down.

7) Option: To increase charge/discharge, put pillows between your legs (see Fig. 8, Component D).

8) On standing, do you feel considerably warmer, freer, more alive? Hold a pillow to your chest if feeling vulnerable. To focus on pleasurable sensations, see Exercise A, Step 9.

Note: doing this exercise is a way to wake up happy in the morning. You can do it in bed with your knees up and feet on the mattress. Or you can do it in the bathroom, seeing yourself in the mirror as your little friend, as you lean against the washbasin for balance!

Exercise C: Laughing (standing)

Laughing is the easiest, most enjoyable and spontaneous way to deepen your breathing. In laughing an energetic wave moves downward through the diaphragm into the lower body. This exercise allows you to laugh strongly without ending up curled on the floor to ease a possible diaphragmatic contraction.

Note: The arching and unarching of the back is considered by some clients to be a body curl, as it follows the same pattern as the extending and curling of the fingers and toes.

1) Immediately before this exercise, do Exercise A to 'ground' yourself, or use traditional grounding so that your feet are firmly on the floor and your legs are vibrating.

2) To stimulate some spontaneous laughter, try to remember a situation when something was so funny that you almost doubled over laughing; or picture yourself as your Natural Child reaching (Exercise B); or as Santa Claus, with a twinkle in your eye; or as a powerful pirate captain.

3) Stand with your knees slightly bent and your hands lightly on your

hips. This will open your throat and chest so that you can laugh more deeply.

4) Thinking of the funny situation, or your excited Child reaching out, or Santa or the pirate captain:

➤ On *inhalation* (see Fig. 13): let your eyes open with excitement, arch your back slightly as your head goes back, and let your mouth open a bit.

➤ On *exhalation* (see Fig. 14): let the laughing sound come out as your eyes close; reverse the arch of your back as your head comes forward, and your chin descends almost to your chest. You may naturally want to begin to bend over as your laugh deepens, in which case your hands need to shift slightly to accommodate this forward movement.

Note: these instructions for inhalation/exhalation are just to help you achieve a full body laugh. If the movements don't come naturally, don't force them – spontaneous laughter is important.

5) Let yourself keep laughing; if the laughing lasts progressively longer on the exhalation, this will deepen your inhalation and help open your throat and chest, which could lead to deeper laughter.

6) When you've had enough, hang down, let your fingertips touch the floor and your legs vibrate. You may wish to continue laughing in this position, which could be more comfortable for your diaphragm.

figure 13

7) On standing again, are you warmer? Eyesight better? More relaxed in shoulders? Breathing more deeply? Feeling more connected in your body?

Revitalized and/or relaxed? More positive about life? Hold a pillow to your chest to protect this new aliveness.

8) If you wish to continue the charging and discharging while standing, just extend and curl your fingers and toes in coordination with your breathing.

9) If you wish to deepen your laughter, begin the laughing again and let your tongue hang out limply from the corner of your mouth, as in Exercise B. When you've had enough, repeat Steps 6, 7 and 8.

10) To focus on perceiving pleasurable sensations, see Exercise A, Step 9.

figure 14

Exercise D: "I can go out to the world ... and come back to myself" (sitting)

Many of us move out into the world from our False Self, with little regard for our deeper unconscious need to protect our Primally Wounded Child. Hence, usually we are not *really* 'out there'; i.e., we may act 'as if' we were involved with others, but we hold back a deeper, more intimate connection, and we may act 'as if' we are 'taking a bite out of life' but we are unconsciously fearful to demand of the world what is rightfully ours, for fear of punishment.

This exercise lets you very slowly, and with gradually increasing degrees of excitation, explore what it means for you to 'go out to the world'; what it means for you to 'come back to yourself'; and how it feels for you to go from one state to the other. (Be aware of the difference between a healthy going into yourself to rest, and more chronic fears of being 'out in the world' and/or of being 'inside yourself'.)

Equipment: A chair without arms, two pillows and some soft fabric for your arches and toes.

1) Sit with feet parallel, hip-width apart, the soft material under your feet so that your foot arches and toes are filled. If desired, put the firm pillow between your back and the chair back.

2) Hold a pillow to your chest, with arms crossed over the pillow and hands curled loosely around the pillow edges. *Keeping your eyes closed*:

figure 15

➤ On *inhalation*, think, "I can go out to the world," and gently extend your fingers and toes.

➤ On *exhalation*, think, "... and I can come back to myself," and gently curl your fingers around the pillow edges and your toes into the soft material.

3) Once you have established the rhythm, what were your emotional and bodily feelings about 'going out into the world'? About 'coming back to yourself'? About being able to go from one state to the other? Is it easier being in yourself than being out in the world? Does your answer surprise you? Were you previously aware that you have a clear choice to be 'in' or 'out'?

4) Repeating the instructions for Step 2, on *inhalation open* your eyes. What did you feel? On *exhalation close* your eyes. What did you feel?

5) With your eyes *closed*, imagine somebody out in the world that you like:

➤ On *inhalation*, while thinking, "I can go out to you," keep your upper arms close to the sides of your body so that your elbows hold the pillow in place, and reach out with your lower arms and hands to that person, as in Fig. 15. Meanwhile arch your back gently by gently pressing your buttocks and shoulders slightly backward, and let your head go also slightly backward. (This will put your chest out more into the world and also add more energetic charge.)

➤ On *exhalation*, while thinking, "... and I can leave you and come back to me," retract your arms and cross them over the pillow again, and curl your fingers over the pillow edges. Meanwhile, gently relax the arch in your back and let your head come slightly forward, as in Fig. 16. (You may find your breathing naturally deepens as you alternate arching and relaxing your back.)

6) Once you have integrated these additional rhythms and energetic charge, did you note that you reached with strong feelings? Were your arms, wrists and hands charged? (Or were they limp, which would have sabotaged your reaching?) Was the act of reaching pleasurable in and of itself?

7) Finally, in addition to the instructions in Step 5, above, add:

➤ On *inhalation*, say *out loud*, "I can go out to you." Did you feel stronger for having said it 'out loud' rather than just 'thinking' it? Did it feel more risky?

➤ On *exhalation*, say *out loud*, "... and I can leave you and come back to me." Did you feel embarrassed about stating out loud that you wanted to come back to yourself – as if you weren't entitled to do that? Or because it would seem offensive and/or selfish?

8) When finished, stand up, hang down, let your legs vibrate, and feel how your feet meet the floor.

9) On standing erect again, you may wish to hold a pillow to your chest. Do you have more clarity about, or respect for, your own feelings of vulnerability? But is your immediate outside world, including people, really so threatening that you need to protect yourself so strongly? Or perhaps you feel your inside world could also be threatening to your False Self identity?

10) To focus on pleasurable sensations, see Exercise A, Step 9.

Exercise E: Opening Out, Gathering In and Keeping (lying on your back)

A basic instinctual organismic movement is to open up, move out to the world to secure what is necessary (e.g., stimulation, food, a mate), gather it in and keep it for oneself. Unfortunately, as infants, our parents may not have encouraged reaching out (e. g., failing to pick us up and feed us when we cried in our crib). As a result, our natural instinctual movements became "tentative, weak and sporadic" Lowen (1967).

Equipment: A mattress or pad, with one end placed against a wall (if possible); three soft bed-pillows; a thin small soft blanket or soft large towel to fill your arches and for your toes to curl into.

1) Lying on your back, put the bottoms of your feet on the mattress with your knees up, 5 or 6 inches apart; slip some soft material (and/or a pillow) under your arches and toes for your toes to curl into; place one pillow on your chest and another under your head to support your neck.

2) On *inhalation*, arch your back slightly (easily done by pressing your buttocks and shoulders lightly into the mattress), let your head go back slightly and leaving the pillow on your chest, fully extend your arms and hands out to the sides, palms facing up – all while thinking, "*I can open out…*;" see Fig. 17.

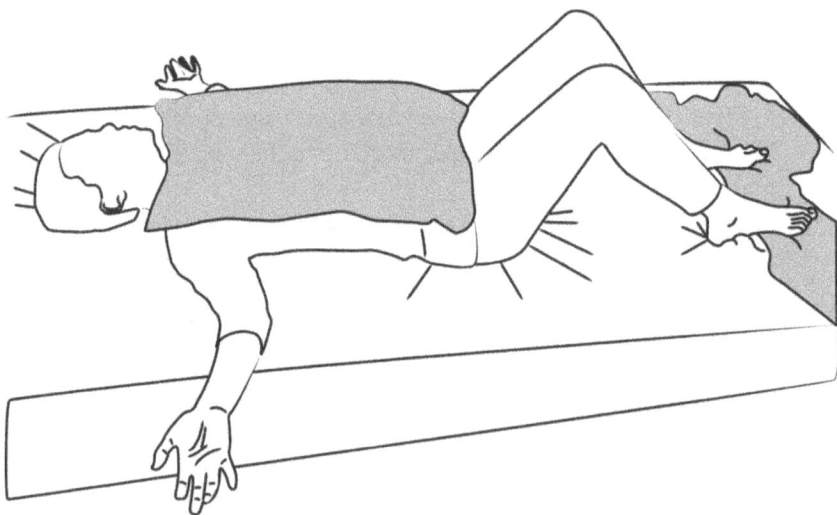

figure 17

3) On *exhalation*, release the arch in your back, let your head come naturally slightly forward (and perhaps your pelvis also), as your arms cross over

the pillow and your fingers curl tightly into the pillow edges – all while thinking, "... *and I can gather in and keep for me;*" see Fig. 18.

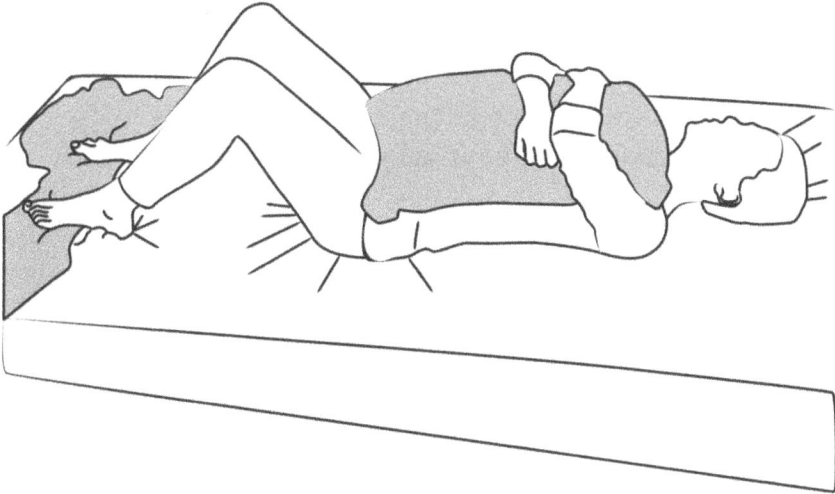

figure 18

4) Once you have established a rhythm, on *inhalation* open your mouth slightly and open your eyes with excitement. On *exhalation*: close your eyes, bring your jaw forward aggressively as you reach out, gather in and keep; you may then also want to clench your jaw and bite down as if you were holding onto something with your teeth.

5) What are your emotional and bodily feelings about being able to open out, to aggressively reach out, bring in and keep for yourself?

6) Continue the process of Steps 2 and 3 until you feel vibrations or involuntary movement. If you wish more vibrations:

➤ Option 1: to feel that you can bring in and keep something also with your legs, the therapist needs to hold two pillows or a cushion positioned between your knees. On inhalation, let your knees go apart (still keeping your feet 5 or 6 inches apart); on exhalation bring your knees together to hold the pillows as tightly as you wish.

➤ Option 2: to accelerate your excitement on the inhalation, keep your eyes open with excitement and let your tongue hang out limply from the corner of your mouth; then, on exhalation let your tongue go in and your lower jaw come forward.

7) When you feel you've had enough excitation and vibratory movement, stop and let yourself rest. Then stand up, bend over, and let the charge come down into your feet and legs.

8) To focus on perceiving pleasurable sensations, see Exercise A, Step 9.

Exercise F: Allowing Fear/Excitation without Being Overwhelmed (lying on your belly)

Our mother's body was the earliest boundary for our very sensitive chest and belly (and also the sensitive insides of our arms and legs), and chest-to-chest contact was fundamental to our feelings of security and safety. Unfortunately, early infant and childhood fears in our contact with our mother and father pulled our energy 'up' and 'in' so that we could not let down to the security and safety that should have been provided by their bodies.

Equipment: a mattress/foam pad, one end against a wall (if available), and 3 soft pillows.

1) As in Fig. 19, lie on your belly, each hand grasping a corner of the mattress or some other soft material. If it is stressful to turn your head to the side, use a pillow so that your neck is relaxed. Your feet should be perpendicular to the mattress, so that the toes can dig in, and the legs can vibrate when stretched.

2) Your therapist places pillows or cushions between your feet and the wall to provide a boundary for your feet.

3) Your therapist now places her hand on your upper back to provide boundary support for the back. If you wish more contact and/or more pressure, your therapist could use both hands and perhaps lean on your back.

4) On *inhalation*: with your eyes *partially open*, extend your fingers and think, "I can feel fear…"

5) On *exhalation*: with your eyes *closed*, curl your fingers while thinking, "… but I can hold myself together" (or what feels best for you, e.g., "… but I'm still safe").

6) What are your emotional and bodily feelings about being able to alternate between feeling fear and yet being able to hold yourself together and/or feel safe?

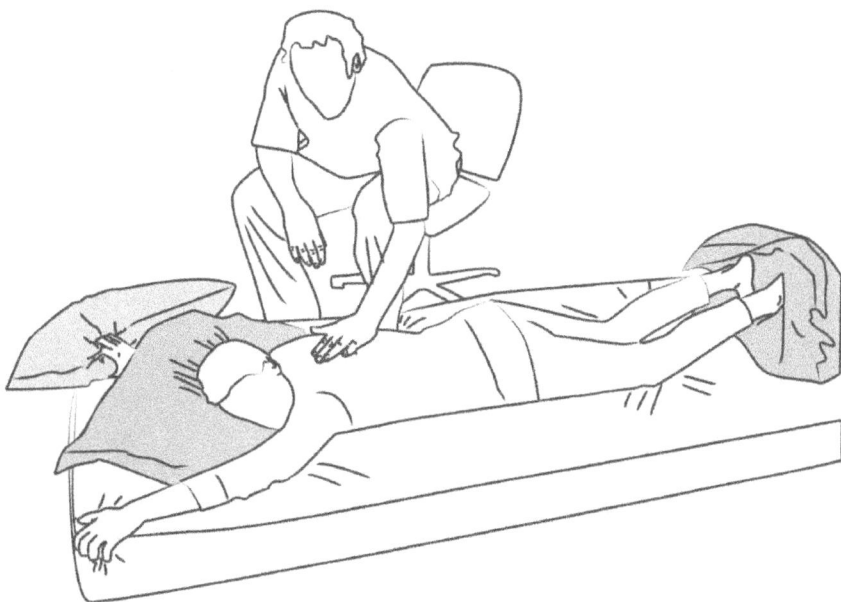

figure 19

7) After approximately 20 breaths, you may begin to feel some energetic flow/vibrations/involuntary movement in your body. If you wish to deepen your process:

➤ On *inhalation:* imagine something (or someone) in your life that you are currently afraid of; extend your fingers and open your eyes wider so that you can feel more fear, and think, "I can feel more fear."

➤ On *exhalation:* close your eyes and think, "… and I can still hold myself together" (or whatever verbalization you choose). However, this time, bring your lower jaw forward to mobilize your aggression to be able to stand the fear.

8) If you wish to deepen your process even further:

➤ On *inhalation:* open your eyes and mouth even wider, and think, "I can feel a lot of fear."

➤ On *exhalation:* say again, "… but I can still hold myself together" (or whatever verbalization you choose) with your jaw forward; however, this time, stretch out the "an" sound of "I can–an–an–an," while progressively tightening the curling of your fingers. Instead of trying to do it all in one exhalation, take little breaths; it will feel like the engine of a sports car when it revs up. (I call this technique Charging/Containing.) You can also experiment with saying "I can–an–an–an" out loud while you exhale.

9) When you've had enough excitement or vibratory movement, stop and let yourself rest briefly. To focus on perceiving pleasurable sensations, see Exercise A, Step 9. Afterwards stand up and let the charge come down into your feet and legs.

IV. Curling Concepts

Polarities and Rhythms

Polarities abound in the Curling exercises. Generally, going to one pole offers risk, charging-up and revitalization; the other pole offers safety, letting down, relaxation. E.g.:

expansion	↔	contraction
opening	↔	closing
inhalation	↔	exhalation
extending	↔	retracting
charging	↔	discharging
arching back	↔	unarching back
out to world	↔	back to self
Body (Natural Child)	↔	Ego (Adult)
letting go of control	↔	building control

The slow steady rhythmical alternation between the two poles of a polarity is very integrating:

➤ Rocking forward and backward to free a car stuck in the mud offers a good analogy to rocking between 'risk' and 'safety'; it frees us muscularly, energetically and psychologically.

➤ Since 'risk' is limited to the time taken to inhale, and 'safety' is regained in the exhalation, our unconscious protective mechanisms (resistance) can relax as the need for protection is being valued and honored.

➤ The regular and very frequent *perception* of both poles *locates* and *strengthens* the Adult (Observing Ego); this lessens resistance and calms the inner turbulence in the subselves that is created by the exercise.

The effectiveness of superimposed rhythms occurs when the basic rhythm of extending and curling is supplemented by another rhythm (e.g., inhalation and exhalation). Adding a third rhythm – e.g., opening and closing the eyes in cadence with the other rhythms – can result in an exponential increase in energetic charge. (A troop of soldiers crossing a bridge does *not* march in step, lest the powerful oscillation thus set up destroy the bridge.) Also, since rhythm is a very important aspect of pleasure, the additional rhythms greatly increase the *pleasurable sensations* from any one exercise.

Why Does Curling Stimulate an Energetic Charge?

Curling's energetic events are possibly a holdover from our simian ancestors in the trees. If you can imagine yourself as an ape swinging from branch to branch in a tree, as long as your fingers, or toes, are wrapped (curled) solidly around a branch, you will not fall and be seriously injured or killed. Thus the closure of the fingers/toes means safety, security and hence the possibility of letting down and relaxing.

However, you need to open your fingers/toes so that you can swing to the next branch and find some food or a suitable mate. Opening your fingers represents some risk but it also has some inherent excitement in the anticipation of being able to secure what you want and find pleasure.

Once we began walking on the earth, it was still important to be able to curl our hands in order to be able to secure and hold onto something, and our toes to be able to curl to hold onto uneven ground. Accordingly, we have a huge number of proprioceptors in our hands and feet. When our hands are filled with soft but firm material so that we can curl our fingers and palms around it, and likewise with the toes and arches of our feet, we can relax and let down – all of which stimulates the expansive, pleasurable flow of energy from the core of our body to the periphery.

Another explanation for the beneficial aspects of Curling is that its movements are similar to nursing at our mother's breast. To open our little fingers is risky but necessary to let our mother's milk come to her nipple; closing our fingers means we possess the breast and, most important, the milk that issues forth. Babies and small children curl their fingers and toes when in pleasure and cats likewise curl their paws.

V. Future Investigations

We saw that Curling exercises involve the slow, steady, rhythmical alternation between the two poles of risk and safety. Could these concepts be incorporated into Bioenergetic maneuvers to help lessen conscious and unconscious resistance, provide more security in 'opening up,' and thus better integrate increases in energetic charge? Can they be used to increase self-awareness, self-possession and thus strengthen overall Adult functioning? Can they be used to deepen perception of the body (with each inhalation) and deepen the perception of pleasurable sensations (with each exhalation)?

Specifically, we saw that letting the tongue hang out limply from the corner of the mouth gives us instant access to our Natural Child core energy and also deepens all feeling; that longitudinal arching and relaxing of the back, in rhythm with our natural breathing pattern, quickly stimulates deeper respiration; that lateral arching and relaxing of the back likewise helps open the heart. Could some of the above maneuvers be integrated into traditional Bioenergetic techniques and thus enrich them?

References

Lowen, A. (1970 Pleasure (New York: Coward-McCann), pp. 220 et seq.
Lowen, A. (1967) Betrayal of the Body (New York: Macmillan), p. 51
Shapiro, B. (2007). Curling: Exercises and Notes (self-published), pp. 31–33

About the Author

Bennett Shapiro, Ph.D. is a member of the IIBA Faculty and teaches in the U.S., Canada and Europe. He has a private practice in Victoria, B.C., Canada. He has written more than 30 papers on various aspects of Bioenergetics and is now extending and consolidating them into six workbooks titled *Explorations in Energizing Psychotherapy.*

Bennett Shapiro, Ph.D.
1542 Prospect Place
Victoria, B.C.
V8R 5X8 Canada
fax: (250) 598–6842
phone: (250) 598–5595
benandmillie@shaw.ca
www.bennettshapiro.com

Fathers are the Dark Matter
of the Psychic Universe

Scott Baum

Summary

This paper explores some of the aspects of fathers' influence on personality development. The author takes the position that significant aspects of that process have been left unexamined, for reasons hypothesized about in the paper. Using personal and clinical material, the author attempts to bring some of those aspects to light.

Keywords: fathers, fathering, men, masculine development

It has been central to my recovery and development of some sense of self to understand my relationship with my father. In the thirty years of intensive personal psychotherapy in which I have engaged, that relationship has only very slowly yielded to my efforts to penetrate its workings. In making that effort I have discovered that the deeper aspects of my and others' relationships with our fathers remain obscured. Trying to penetrate that obscurity for myself and with my patients, I feel like I am trying to enter a territory in the map indicated by a large dark space–*terra incognita*. Besides the personal meaning to each person of this critical force in our lives, it is also a profoundly significant shaping force in our communal lives and in the formation of the culture that enfolds us.

If the relationship dynamics between fathers and children are as obscured as I think they are, then attempting to truly evaluate the effect fathers have on our children is a very difficult task. Specifically I mean here the psychodynamic and somatopsychic effects. These effects then relate to everything a person does, of course, but they are often not as visible or obvious as behaviors are. I am trying to get at the formative effects, the kinds of things one sees in response to continuous energetic impact. Dynamic forces that result in accretal, erosive, structuring reactions, that make people who they are at the deepest levels, and are often obscured from view.

As I grappled with this problem of the unseen effect of fathers, it occurred to me that it resembles the cosmological theory of 'dark matter'. This theory attempts to acknowledge that the visible and measurable (to us), mass in the universe only accounts for a fraction of the gravity known to exist. The mass must be there, but is unseen, hence dark matter. Similarly, as I will attempt to show here, the effect of fathers on the somatopsychic development of children, is clearly demonstrated in our clinical work, and in the world around us, but hardly viewed directly.

Current literature and discussion on fathers and our effect on families and society in our functioning as fathers seems to me to focus on three broad areas. In the first (not in order of priority) the focus is on the significance to the development of the personality of children, especially sons, when fathers are absent or occupy only a peripheral role in our children's lives. This is an area of social behavior that has undergone significant change in the last twenty-five years. Seen in such seemingly small matters as diaper changing tables in men's restrooms, this change is huge; however, as I will suggest below, not entirely for the good. In works like *Raising Cain* (Kindlon & Thompson, 2000), the argument is made that the emotional limitations we see so often in boys come very substantially out of relationships with their fathers characterized by distance, coldness or detachment, or criticality unrelieved by softness or empathy or compassion from the fathers.

In the psychoanalytic literature, as exemplified by Benjamin (1986) the father is seen as a force helping to pull the child out of the symbiotic orbit with mother. In this respect he is an exciting object who represents the outside (of the family) world. He acts as facilitator of the developmental thrust toward greater autonomy in the child, and as a counterweight to the regressive pull of the mother's enveloping caring and sympathy.

Feminist theory (Silverstein, 1996) offers yet another viewpoint. It critiques both the inadequate attention to the social and psychological effects of current fathering behaviors, and the tendency to overvalue fathers as providers, and authorities. Seen from this perspective, fathers' roles and behaviors have not changed sufficiently in the social context to adequately alter the misogynistic patterns of power distribution.

Each of these views has substantial merit, and each addresses a significant aspect of the dynamics that organize the relationship between fathers and children. Feminist theorists, in particular, do not shy away from identifying and decrying the prevalence of abuse and exploitation so often present in the relationships between men and our dependents. Yet in all of these views (and I do not pretend here to do them justice in the complexity and broadness of their insights) I find something missing. Something about the inner workings of this relationship that affects us all. Something that is best understood through the investigation afforded by in-depth psychotherapy.

In my search to illuminate these forces of fathering, I realized I could do no better than look to my own experience for insight. Then I might be able to match my experience up with observation and data collected from others' experience. Unavoidably, this methodology would introduce a bias, even a skew, into my findings, since my experience with fathering has been so devastating. But if, even with that skew, my findings resonated with other data, from others, or from the culture which we all breathe and assimilate, then perhaps there are generalizations to be made. These generalizations are likely to apply directly to only a proportion of men, perhaps especially those of us who end up seeking psychotherapeutic help. But personal and professional experience over many years tells me that these generalizations also apply to aspects of our culture as human beings that are pervasive, often subtle, and significant in their effects.

In fact, as I tried desperately to understand my negative feelings and behaviors as a father, and deepen my sensitivity to the impact I was having, I asked for help. But little help with this issue was available, and ultimately I had to find out for myself, using feedback especially from those most affected. Those who know me well, or have read my work, know that I live in an internal emotional underworld of great darkness, where I experience profound negativity and hopelessness. Surely this has influenced greatly my understanding of what transpires between fathers and our children, still I believe I have seen things and seen them in a way that can be generalized and is relevant beyond my unique circumstances.

Professionally, I think we have to shake ourselves out of the torpor of the modern view of psychotherapist as a facilitator of adaptation, because it so often can be based on denial. In this case the denial is born of many of the same dynamics that are frequently intrinsic to the fathering process. If we make it our project to examine the dynamics of fathering in society, wherever that analysis may take us, we will all have to challenge the denial and anxiety this analysis can cause.

It is not our role to tell people what their purpose in therapy is. But we must be prepared to see a person's experience as clearly, and without distortion – especially the impact of chronic abuse against the self – as we can. We must be prepared to challenge our patients and ourselves with a depth of analysis and conscious experience of the dynamics of fathering. That analysis may run counter to conventional views of benevolent paternity. It may well directly oppose cherished political, social, and psychological beliefs about benign patriarchy and the healthiness of the dependency.

Starting with my personal data about my father, and father figures, and then myself as a father, my discoveries, however disturbing, may shine a light on much broader phenomena that affect many people, although perhaps in less destructive ways than they affected me. Whether in less destructive ways or not, the fact that these dynamics, forces, and processes are at work in many of us is significant. It is significant not only in the ways they affect each of us in the development and unfolding of our individual psychologies, but also in the ways our psychologies interact collectively.

I grew up idolizing my father, as many men do. It is true that my idolization was conditioned and thus intensified by the fact that he saved me from a very disturbed, very destructive mother. She was a dead person inside, he was not. He made himself appear to be, and in comparison to her, at least in my eyes, he was, the sane one. I clung to him desperately as we three traversed the first nine years of my life. Initially, after he left her when I was one-and-a-half years old, the custodial arrangement called for twice-weekly visits by my father – which, as far as I can remember, he kept to faithfully. Each time he came to get me over the first five years, I felt like I was being released from jail. And each return was despair and terror. He rescued me by maintaining his tie to me, even through kidnappings on both sides. Eventually, after a court-ordered six month and six month split, we left our hometown, and then the country, thereby assuring that my mother, who was not pursuing her custodial rights very aggressively, would be unable to reach me.

I offer this history in part to give some sense of how difficult it has been for me to examine my father's behavior as a predator, and a perpetrator of abuse. My father encouraged my idealizations of him. He was different from other fathers. He was open, and open to emotions, he was not afraid to touch, or of sexuality. He was a charismatic leader, and I was his living demonstration of the way to raise an emotionally healthy, assertive, secure child. People believed all this of him, and followed him. Although some, like my wife, saw fairly quickly – long before I did – how limited he was, how much of his interaction was filled with contempt and superiority, and a deep-seated need for control.

It is important to share this because what my father did, although extreme in its own way, is what men do characteristically. We overwhelm and intimidate, we say things with emphaticness and absoluteness, and we show contempt for those who do not yield, who do not submit to us. Yes, of course, some men do not behave that way–all the time. But it is part of our indoctrination and enculturation as men. In fact it is an intrinsically double-binding communication all men I know have experienced: "in the playground don't tolerate any put down or domination–fight! In the classroom tolerate and submit to any humiliation and keep still and quiet". If you look at us men as we are organized vertically, from most intimate to most surface, I do not think you will find many of us capable of softness, resiliency, and receptivity across the different levels of interaction from least to most intimate.

At some point the requirement that we be rigid and refuse to be subordinated will arise. This can happen in the smallest ways, as I know too well. Being offered suggestions about how to do something, for example, or being asked to explain something we are doing can be enough to trigger a defensive raising of the hackles. We are ready to fight, very often responding to an over-imagined internalized humiliating person, and then responding to the wave of humiliation that has swept all other sensations before it, the need to fight to the death for honor and self-esteem taking priority over anything else. We have little equipment to cope with that imperative to fight except by enacting it or displacing it. So, we can fight, or we can yield and displace the negativity elsewhere, to those dependant on, or vulnerable to us. We have little, or no, training in how to meet and negotiate with each other, how to be receptive, and how to maintain our integrity even in the face of hostility actually directed at us from the outside, without precipitating violence of one kind or another.

I am talking about the general enculturation of men here, not about any specific man or exception to the rule. I acknowledge those may exist. But as

I try to think about such a man specifically, I cannot name one. It is not a question of perfection. It is rather, recognition that the specific character flaws that men evince, even when we do the right things and espouse the right positions, have great relevance for how we run the world. And make no mistake, we run the world.

This, I believe relates very directly to our work as therapists. We have studied extensively the intricacies of children's relationships with their mothers. We have, as a field, correctly identified the significance of attachment as a basic constituent of human experience and development. But we continue to see it largely as a phenomenon in early childhood taking place between mother and child. Freud, in his emphasis on Oedipal processes, makes it clear that what happens between children and their fathers matters. Indeed it does; but it is very hard to study. It is threatening to us all, as members of this culture, to risk the dangers of raising consciousness, our own and others on this subject. What is the real impact of the formation of identity through the identification with and submission to an intimidating figure? We see the evidence of the effects of this process all around us, in the mix of idealization and repulsion from mobsters, example.

Were we to study the personality shaping dynamics of these processes more closely, we would, I think, have to face the severity of the negative impact fathers have individually, and as representatives of cultural forces and ideologies. We would have to deconstruct the power dynamics of relationships in a society in which one gender predominates over another in the distribution of power. Doing this would open to revelation (and analysis) the intrapsychic, the energetic, and the characterological impact of that fact.

Right now men, as fathers, are seen largely as the facilitators of separation from the regressive infantile clinging to mother. We are not seen as primary attachment figures who are competitive with mothers and siblings, and who demand a most profound loyalty and submissiveness to our needs and demands. Not seeing this clearly, leaves us unable to study the subtle manipulations and collusions, as well as the outright dominations that reflect the workings of the system.

It is my position that it is mistaken to believe that enabling, or even insisting, that men and fathers become more available, or even more emotionally responsive, will change things. Rather, only if we analyze and modify the underlying power system to which we all subscribe, and in the case of men, give up our privileged status, can there be adequate space created for new things to develop. Giving up privilege is difficult. I, for one, find it very hard. Of course this is tied up with my own narcissistic desperation. But it is also part of my enculturation as a man. Here I am talking about the privileges connected to power and the exercise of power.

Modern feminist theory has changed our view of relationship patterns in psychotherapy and in the world. The relational model of psychotherapy process finds many of its originating concepts in the feminist view of relationship as an egalitarian, mutual, co-created process in which the psychotherapeutic and democratic ideal of even the smallest voice being heard can be realized. In this view the man and the father have to be more than the figure who assists the child to emerge from the mother's orbit for the purposes of separation and the development of autonomy. He would have to become the co-creator, with an autonomous and self-realized mother, of a mutually dependent matrix. In this model, autonomy is grounded in successful dependency, the kind of dependency one sees in mother-child relationships wherein the mother supports and facilitates individuation and separation because she loves her child, and her or his burgeoning mastery and independence.

I remember a colleague, a bioenergetic therapist, and a man who had worked on himself, and had an enlightened view of sexism in the culture. But he also felt that men were being characterized unfairly, that the pendulum had swung too far in identifying men as chauvinistic and over-powerful. I could hear his resentment at having to accept the burden of being a part of the privileged class. He felt wronged by women, and he felt that the view of men as destructive in our superiority, and as the ruling group was exaggerated and persecutory. This was happening hardly after the women's movement had emerged, and the true nature of the oppressive system women live in was just being limned. It informed me how limited the open space would be for the honest acknowledgement of our participation as members of the ruling group, and how hard it would be for us to give up our privileged position in society, which exists even when we feel oppressed because of personal or social realities. This experience gave me some clue about how hard it would be to redress the harm of lifetimes of inequality, prejudice, and discrimination.

At the same time, my friend's distress with the new identities being offered and demanded of men points to an important fact. Within the family – people often say – they saw the wife and mother have the power, and therefore be the dominant figure. In this frequently described configuration, it is argued that it is really the mother who is powerful to the children, with the father a weak, or secondary character. It certainly can be true that in any particular familial constellation, this is the way things are within the family. But the family does not exist in a social vacuum. And the children in the family, while young and immature, are not oblivious to the social environment in which their family functions. In that environment, by any measure, it is men who predominately control things. Even where women are the actual holders of authority, the system we all have to adapt to is a system evolved over many generations to correspond to the values predominately espoused by men. In that system the values espoused by men make us the ultimate repositories of authority.

Our focus as a profession on the importance of the interpersonal field, and the significance in people's lives of attachment, has brought us to a recognition of the formative meaning of a child's early relationships. In particular, theory and research over many decades has brought into view the prominent meaning and impact of the child's relationship with her or his mother. This focus remedied some of the neglect of the mother as an important figure in her own right in a child's intrapsychic and interpersonal life. But there is even now still something of a feeling for me that we view the mother's function as preparing a child (especially boys) for the important tasks of entering and controlling in the real world, and those functions and activities are mediated by men, so the mother remains a subsidiary figure (a regent to the king) hovering in the background, hopefully a nurturing or benign presence, sustaining the person in his contention with the world, but not herself really a player in it. Most children in our culture experience a version of a scenario in which the mother is in charge of the household and childrearing, but there is always authority reposing in the father to overrule or veto her authority. When this is not done by frank overpowering, is often done by disparagement and sabotage.

This view enables a denial on all our parts of the significance of the paternal role, both as father and representative of the masculine identity in society. We pretend that men do not run things, and that understanding our patients' dynamics and experience does not require that we see the impact that denial of that has on them. It is because of this that modern discussion of the role of fathers focuses so much on the question of the father's presence or absence in the child's physical reality. The focus should be much more on what the father's presence is, in whatever form, in a child's intrapsychic and somatopsychic reality. We know very well as clinicians that distance and remove and reserve can enhance a person's aura of power. We know this from the evocativeness of the analyst's abstinence and apparent detachment. Mothers, as a group, rarely feel such reserve or abstinence is appropriate or acceptable, and it is usually a requirement and expectation that they be engaged and hands-on. Fathers often engage in abstinence reflexively as an expression of power facilitated by greater emotional unresponsiveness.

I watch as David twists and turns in the couple therapy with his wife. A man in his early sixties he is devoted to his wife, and to a vision of them as a couple. The vision includes love, recognition, appreciation, affection, and an egalitarian framework in which both are equal and equally valued. Many times she attempts to show him how he reflexively diminishes her and her position. He's a man whose convictions are strong about politics and morality. He has worked hard to become more open, more peace-loving, to recover from a childhood of denigration and belittlement. A man of many talents, he can build and repair most anything, he teaches and performs as an artist, and he is vigorous, athletic and virile. Each time his wife, Sarah, tries to tell him about her feelings of depreciation at his hands, he replies with a moment's receptivity. Then, driven by a deep sense of humiliation and shame, and a profound narcissistic defensiveness, he launches into a recriminatory justification of himself. Has he not done so much to change? Has he not done so much to improve their lives? How can she insult him so, with these terrible accusations? He hammers her until she falls silent.

Finally, feeling I know him well enough, and the issues all too well, I enter the fray. I say his wife is telling him that he has no heart for her. At first taken aback, he summons himself up, indignant. But she supports my view consistently, willing to risk his wrath, and her own disappointment, to face the truth in her and him. We go through the cycle many times. She tells him he disrespects her, in small and big ways, a thousand times a day. She tells him that she is becoming resigned to the possibility that their relationship will not be what she had hoped, although it is so much, even now. He pulls himself up in outrage and hurt—what about his side of the story? With my help she battles back his attempts to break her down, and then he softens, and the truth of his desire to do the right thing emerges. As does his vision of himself as a man like the man she wants him to be. And the severity of his limitations in his capacity, and perhaps motivation, to become that man, to the best of his ability comes into view. He softens, then, and tells her with evident sincerity of his desire, and intention to be the kind of man who truly loves, honors, and respects his wife, as partner, collaborator, and witness.

I know this pattern of David's all too well, because it is mine also. I know it as husband, and as father, and I see it in the men around me. Its constituents are a basic competitive disrespect for others, and a need to be superior. It is based on a fundamental limitation in empathy, in the ability to experience another person's reality, *and* to value it as much as one's own. Basic training in relatedness for men is accomplished through humiliation and embarrassment. Men don't refrain from asking for directions because we are too stupid to know when we are lost, but because we anticipate the ridicule from the gas station attendant when it is revealed that we have been driving on the street we have been looking for all along.

The inculcation of these attitudes is a basic aspect of the socialization of men, handed down from father, coach, male teachers, public figures, and of course mothers, to male children. And so to some extent cannot be avoided by any of us. In some cases, like mine, the cumulative effect of the personal and social forces at work destroys the capacity for compassion and love, leaving only the malevolent forces behind with any significant visceral reality. The only option for goodness then becomes a set of principles to believe in and follow, even without the visceral emotionally based conviction to go with them. The visceral emotional ground for empathy, compassion, and healthy submission to the needs and welfare of others, is not built. Rather the male child learns to despise these processes and feelings as sissified, they feminize and humiliate him.

It is hard for people to accredit this view I have of myself, but it gives me a very distinctive vantage point from which to view the impact of fathers on our children, on our wives or partners, and thus, ultimately on society as a whole. The negativity I see, endemic to the psychology of men, is often subtle. There are many rationalizations for its expression, some offered by the perpetrators, some by the victims. But there exists an underlying competitiveness, driven by unconscious and exquisite sensitivity to dynamics of power and dependency. The acknowledgement of dependency, for men, is to be denied at all costs because dependency always entails humiliation; humiliation of a kind that will require either revenge or suicide. Those feelings are enacted and expressed in various forms, such as retaliation, defiance or sabotage, or splitting and identification with the aggressor.

Coping with these interpersonal and intrapsychic forces requires strong action. Disparagement, devaluation, contempt, envy, dismissiveness, and derogation, are leveled at one's opponents, those who would defeat and vanquish us. And with equal ferocity at those who hold us in their hands by virtue of the vulnerability engendered in us by our dependency on them. Given the pervasiveness of these attitudes, the force of the action enacting them, and the power differential that most of the time exists between perpetrator and victims, victims are left with little choice but to blunt consciousness. Or being conscious, to form various counter defenses of ultimate superiority, or rationalizations and accommodations to the abuse which assert impermeability to the toxins. How many times do therapists hear the mother or wife describe the father and husband as just another child in the house, when it is evident she is being devalued and even mistreated? To remain conscious, to acknowledge vulnerability, and to understand the nature of the power dynamics, leaves one with little choice but to fight for identity, for value, for one's psychic and spiritual life.

This is the situation I find myself in. Despite appearances to the contrary–my father was a very successful body-oriented psychotherapist for the last third of his life–he carried dramatic versions of these basic attitudes of men that I have described. When combined with the effects of my earliest childhood when I was exposed to an even more unvarnished version of evil in the environment around my mother, I have had little inner experience of the reality of goodness to bring to bear to counter the hateful and malevolent attitudes infused and grown within me. This reality meant that it took years of agonizing, very difficult work for me to see the true force of these attitudes within me, and their expression. It would undoubtedly have taken much more time, or not even happened at all, had my wife not insisted on fighting tooth-and-nail against my imposition of these destructive patterns of behavior and expression on her and on our family.

In the end, I have discovered that the most I can do is participate in the formation of a space in which my wife and children can be protected, as much as is possible, from the unchallenged expression of the toxic attitudes and affects of merciless competitiveness and devaluation I embody with such force and ferocity. So, in my case, being more available was certainly not the gift we imagine when we talk about fathers' greater involvement in the lives of their families. In some ways my capacity to contain and restrain the expression of these feelings comes too late, severe damage has been done to those closest to me. One can see that, for example, in my wife's having to spend so much of her emotional and psychic energy setting limits on my acting out, or recovering her ground after being mind-fucked, sufficiently to assert reality and demand I acknowledge what has happened. And I can see it in my son's expression of feeling himself without a self, having had his selfness attacked and decimated, and then identifying with my rigid, controlling demanding-ness and assertions of superiority. My daughter, while spared some of the devaluation and competitiveness, had to take distance from me, and my wife. From my wife because her decision to take care of me made her less available to her children than her love of them would have otherwise directed her to be. From me, among other reasons, to cope with the assimilating force of my identification with her athleticism (a common problem in men with athletically gifted children), even though I was attempting to control it. These are only examples, of course, of what was a pervasive set of dynamics, but represent some of those dynamics related specifically to the issues under discussion here. It is painful to contemplate the tragic disruption of the very loving feelings between my wife and my children, in both directions, so severely deformed by these attitudes and feelings. This pattern of alienation due to hostile and devaluing attitudes is to some extent endemic to men as fathers. Where moth-ers embody and express the same attitudes, it often reveals elements of these same dynamics as they have been structured into the culture.

In some ways, my awareness of these negative attitudes and behaviors, and my intention and struggle to restrain their expression comes just in time in my own family. Because there is yet much which can be preserved, and allowed to develop. But the truth of the dynamics, the actions, the feelings and the structures, powered and engendered by these attitudes can only be ignored at great peril to all of us. This is true in my family, in *the* family, as representative of the basic emotional and social home of us all, and in society as a whole, an outgrowth of the family.

It is a basic conviction in bioenergetic theory, as it is in many humanistic philosophies, that once consciousness is raised, and emotional obstacles re-moved, compassion and empathy will flow relatively unobstructed. On a very basic practical level this seems to me incorrect. Compassion, empathy, and sensitivity are all attributes, which in their deployment improve with practice and refinement. So, just clearing the way for their emergence, while necessary, is not sufficient for them to become well-used and sophisticated elements in human relatedness. These capacities must be honed, and dovetailed with skillfulness in communication and expression, to reach a person's potential for goodness and right behavior.

In fact, focusing on the aspect of relational attunement in meaningful interactions, including in one's sexual life, which is so central to a Bioenergetic view of life, means getting to know oneself and the other. Going through strong, cathartic events is part of that experience. In this respect, both sexuality and aggression are central to the development of men. Clearly, the focus in bioenergetics on the full experience of one's sexual self is critical to one's development, but not as a vehicle for discharge of pent-up energy from stimulation, as much as a vehicle to know oneself through the matrix of relationship with another.

The focus on discharge takes us back to the primitive and the unrefined, and can lead to objectification of the self and the other. This is something we see often in modern representations of sexuality in the culture. This focus on discharge can be useful as a tool to open closed structures and dulled sensations, but it is not an end in itself. A more desirable end is to develop the capacity for self-directed and self-sustaining autonomous growth and development in our ability to be in contact with ourselves, others and reality.

The same is true with respect to aggression. One unaddressed issue in the life of men is the inevitably life-altering experience we go through when we go to war, whether government directed, or part of the culture of the streets we grow up in. We maintain a fiction, clearly pointed out by David Grossman (1996) that one can try to, and even kill, another, or be threatened with death, and not be permanently affected. The effect on us of being threatened with murder, or attempting it on another, is likely to be in the direction of greater hardness and insensitivity. The logical end to profound devaluation and competitive control is killing.

My experience of the terror of being threatened with death as a very young child; and with penetration, physical and psychic; and with identity annihilation through manipulation and torture; and feeling the feeling and the consequences for me of murderous rage, a compassionless urge for revenge, tells me that even healthy, solid, grown men are challenged to the edge of madness when they are required to kill. What happens to children exposed to this level of inhumanity and horror, even if it is only in the body of someone they love–their father?

And what happens when these same forces and feelings are acted out in the crucible of the family? Even if a hand is never raised to another, only words, tones, looks, and attitudes are conveyed.

It might be argued that this view is so skewed it sees only the most egregious cases of fatherhood in this culture. Things are much more moderate than they seem here. Both my own experience, and the popular culture tell me that this is probably not true. I coached youth athletics for ten years, and I was involved in the administration in the administration of those programs with men who are, as a group, among the most enlightened and aware men I know. I saw very clearly the ferocity with which these attitudes of deadly competition, and the drive for supremacy, coupled with characterological and cultural desensitization, still prevail even among those men who deplore them.

The focus in popular culture on fathers – e.g. in the Simpsons, Family Guy, Home Improvement, All in the Family, and the like – reveals them on the whole to be fatuous, bloated, self-important, vain, oblivious and destructive people, with fragile egos, immense social power, and yet given the undying love and devotion of their dependents. Think of characters from Ralph Kramden to Homer Simpson. The proliferation of such characters right now, I believe, is a way for young people to deal with their relative helplessness in a world dominated by such people, by ironically embracing and laughing at them. But I think the underlying truth is that these characters represent a truth about the state of fathers and fathering in the world today.

Raising our consciousness, opening ourselves to feeling, and enhancing capacity for cathartic experiences is not enough. To expose the destructive dynamics embedded in the current methods of fathering and becoming a man, requires acknowledging that fathers' effect must be like the "dark matter" I talk about in my title, in order to explain its form. It is not measurable because it is not visible to us, but it must exist because of the immense gravitational force it exerts. A force which is believed in current cosmological theory to determine the shape of the universe as we know it to be. A force, though not visible, many times greater than that exerted by what is visible. Similarly, in the world, men dominate. Children, while immature, can see what is there to be seen, and even if they cannot see it, they feel the inexorable effects of the forces at work.

Looking to the past to find for ourselves a way to embody the lessons of empathic attunement and subjective relating will not succeed. As best I know, given the known record of human history, we are more available now than ever before for a social system prioritizing relatedness and equality. Attaching priority to relational attunement and interconnectedness requires the development of a new kind of person. It may be that this is not the natural human form, or it is for too few humans, despite what research and belief conclude. We may have to make it a specific project to develop ourselves and humans into such people. It is not the job of therapists to tell our patients what kind of people to turn into. But in order to be maximally available for choices that test the range of human possibility, do we not have to have as full and as deep an understanding of the impact on our patients, and ourselves, of fathers, and men, as we can possibly have? And with that awareness be willing to face and facilitate a change in consciousness and behavior in our patients, in ourselves, and in the world in which we live.

References

Benjamin, J. [1986]: The Alienation of Desire: Women's Masochism and Ideal Love. The Analytic Press, Hillsdale NJ, 113–38

Grossman, D. [1996]: On Killing. Little Brown and Co., New York

Kindlon D. & Thompson, M. [2000]: Raising Cain. Random House, New York

Silverstein, L. [1996]: Fathering is a Feminist Issue. Psychology of Women Quarterly, 20, 3–37

About the Author

Scott Baum, Ph.D., ABPP, is a clinical psychologist practicing and living in New York City. He is on the faculty of the New York Society for Bioenergetic Analysis, and a member of the International Faculty of the IIBA.

Scott Baum, Ph.D.
711 West End Avenue (1AN)
New York, NY 10025
USA
docsbpsych@aol.com

"If You Turned into a Monster"

Transformation through Play: A Body-Centered Approach to Play Therapy. By Dennis McCarthy

Book Review and Reflections by *Vincentia Schroeter*

This book about play therapy with children combines the energy- oriented techniques of Alexander Lowen with the attention to symbolism of Carl Jung.

How is it relevant to us? Many Bioenergetic therapists are looking for techniques that are applicable to children and this book has many clinical cases full of specific Bioenergetic diagnostic and treatment techniques for children.

Why is it in the journal? Dennis McCarthy was in supervision with Lowen in the 1980's. When McCarthy would begin giving him diagnostic background on the child client, Lowen insisted the author tell him how the children moved in order to assess the blocks in the energetic flow. McCarthy states that this way of observing became his most powerful diagnostic tool, and an effective means of working with the child toward reclaiming their natural spiritedness. Parts of the first chapter in his book were previously published in our clinical journal, Bioenergetic Analysis 8, 1, pp. 99–105.

I used to think it was not useful to do Bioenergetics with children because they still need the character defenses they are erecting in order to cope with the family system they are still growing up in. However, McCarthy believes that if you help the child, along with motivating the parents to get help, a shift toward health can occur both in the child and in the parents, which can transform those negative family dynamics. Through out the book the emphasis is in the specific treatment of the child, and not on the parents. In fact, the parents in his book, seem to respond well, just to the suggestion from the author that they become more gentle, or understanding, or tolerant, or less abusive, less dependent, or whatever they need to better the situation at home. I found this unrealistic from my experience. While parents often wish to improve they are also attached to their defenses and offer resistance to change. This is not explored in this book. The author gives a rationale for his stance in chapter 14, where he admits that parents have been, "conspicuously absent from these pages." He goes on to say that he wishes to illuminate the power of a child to transform on a psychic and energetic level through play therapy.

Theorists often advocate treating only the child, as did Melanie Klein, who developed the technique of play therapy and ignored the parents to focus on the role of fantasy in the life of the child. She believed that children through play and drawings projected their feelings in the therapeutic sessions revealing infantile fantasies and anxieties. Through her methods an attempt was made to relieve the child of guilt by having them direct toward the therapist the aggressive and oedipal feelings they couldn't express toward their parents. (1) John Bowlby, who developed attachment theory, emphasized the actual history of the relationship and focused on the attachment patterns in the family. Following Bowlby's lead and congruent with attachment theory, are current theorists and clinicians whose techniques involve both the parent and child. A few of the notable ones are Alicia Lieberman's "parent-child psychotherapy", Stanley Greenspan's "floor-time" and Robert Marvin's "circle of security". (2) Having taken workshops with all three of these child psychotherapists and having done research based on attachment theory myself (3) I have not been a proponent of the more Kleinian style of treating the child without the parent. So it was with some skepticism that I approached reading McCarthy, who treats the child and not the parents.

McCarthy feels that "too little is known and understood about what a child is, separate from their family system."(p. 137) He feels we overemphasize the power of the parent, and boldly states, "Most of the children I work with have made huge changes often with their parents making very few." (p. 138)

Whether you insist that the parents must be treated for a child to improve, as Dan Siegel promotes in his book, PARENTING FROM THE INSIDE OUT, (4), or you believe a child can prosper without much parental shift, McCarthy's book will show you case after case of children using their own energy to transform into healthier and happier beings. I admit I was surprised and inspired by these cases where each child wielded the power, fairly independent from parental influence, to make their life better.

I will review some of the aspects he taps into in his chapters full of diverse children he has helped. One of his first requests to a new child client is, "Draw a picture of what you would look like if you turned into a monster." (p. 19) Here he shows his Lowenian roots as he says, "Children come to therapy with monstrous feelings-monstrous grief, monstrous rage, monstrous longing."(p. 20).

McCarthy says that from early on we dream and imagine monsters, and writes about the importance of monsters both as an untamed energy and an unintegrated symbol. "Children speak in the immediate language of the body and the imagination, their symbols being a composite of the two, body and mind" (p. 29). This emphasis in chapter two, of the importance of symbol reminds me of Guy Tonella's paper in this journal, where he writes about the importance of the representational in our self development. Guy also writes about the interface of representational and energy, which McCarthy also deals with in chapter three.

In chapter three we go from symbol to energy and follow treatment of children over time as they transform their monsters mostly through sandtray scenes that they create. The author works with the anger children manifest with the Bioenergetic understanding and processes of charging, meeting a block, discharging and integration.

Chapter four is entitled, "Energy" and is a clear exposition of Bioenergetics. McCarthy mentions what is lost when therapists he supervises do not understand the Reichian concept of pulsation, which the author describes clearly in his work with children. All the cases in this chapter are based completely on Lowen's work, as he works through the Bioenergetic lens of energy, pulsation, grounding, the importance of expression, and the importance of active discharge.

"The Power of No" is the title of chapter five and is full of familiar Lowenian concepts such as needing to say no before you can say yes, and that self-assertion is the basis of self-identity. McCarthy states that most of the children he has worked with are either unable to say no, or unable not to say no. (p. 62). Children whose defense systems organize around saying no loudly in an oppositional or provocative way express it by being disruptive, stubborn, resistant or violent. As McCarthy explains it, they are stuck and in pain because "no" has lost it's discriminatory function, and therapy involves surrendering the battle once it becomes safe to do so. What kind of monsters do you think these children create? I found it fascinating that kids who say no too easily make monsters that are not violent or grotesque but helpful. McCarthy tells us why, "For them it is the noble, heroic part of the self that is repressed and turned into something conflictual." (p. 63). This chapter ends with the case of Michael, a six year old still in diapers. The situation is complex, the therapy is presented clearly and the outcome is strongly effective.

In chapter six the author writes about his supervision with Lowen and also states his belief that transformation through play may be "more monumental" (than adult transformation), because it may spare the child years of internal struggle and pain." (p. 75). This is a compelling reason for putting suffering children into therapy.

The rest of the chapters are equally as interesting and I recommend the book for Bioenergetic therapists, and any other therapists interested in new ways of understanding and transforming the lives of children through these methods.

In mythology, monsters have the power to destroy and create. They provoke change on the heroes and heroines in stories. By forcing change they make things happen, they make life happen. After reading this book I was eager to ask a child to draw a monster and here is what happened:

My eight year old niece was spending the night at my house by herself without her older sisters for the first time. I asked if she would participate with me in this experience and she agreed. I asked, "If you turned into a monster, what you would look like?" She eagerly got to work drawing a green growling monster with horns and holes all over it's body. She named it, "Arain" and told me all about her.

> "She steals anything; she eats anything. She has a horrible singing voice. When she talks she has a growly voice. She eats people, leaves the bones and throws their heart into the ocean." (In the drawing she has added three hearts and made an arrow directed away from Arain and made an energetic gesture with her own arms of throwing the hearts away.) "If she eats a heart she will die, and that is the only way you can kill her. She will eat anything but hearts and avocadoes. The devil doesn't have a heart and she belongs to the devil. If she eats a heart she will be gone forever, destroyed, her spirit won't even be alive. She used to be an angel but she listened to the devil. She hates people. Tonight she is going to steal the whole grocery store and eat the manager."

I wrote all this down as she was talking. She appeared somewhat scared of Arain as we took a walk, and she put out both arms with wrists bent and said, "I feel protected by God from Arain." She made growly voices and practiced symbolically throwing hearts into the ocean. She began laughing and appeared relaxed after that discharge of energy. When we came back in the house she went over to her drawing of Arain, painted a black dress on her and put her in my room on a footstool. She had me call her mother so she could tell her all about Arain, warning her Arain might rob a grocery store tonight, then told me to send her Mom all the information I had written about Arain. Then she got ready for bed, asked me to read her three books and she fell sound asleep for the night. When she left the next day, she took her Polly Pocket dolls, but left her monster, Arain.

I am less interested in interpreting the meaning of the story she told than I am in the fact that she drew eagerly and without hesitation created an elaborate narrative for her monster. The monster possessed aspects she found scary and she expressed the anger energetically by growling and throwing hearts away making her tiny voice loud and her little arms powerful. She appeared more self possessed afterwards and able to demand a comforting structure for bedtime.

I am reminded of what McCarthy says Lowen told him in supervision, "Just tell me how they move!" (p. 72). Lowen would say this emphatically when McCarthy would attempt to present a child by focusing on pathology or diagnosis. Through this Bioenergetic influence as well as Jungian influence Dennis McCarthy has written a book describing his thirty years of work helping children transform their private pain into energized personal power. It was fun to read and I got absorbed in the stories. The book is a clear exposition of effective treatment and I recommend it for the fascinating journey through cases with specific details and impressive results.

References

McCarthy, D. (2007) "If You Turned into a Monster" Transformation through Play: A Body-Centered Approach to Play Therapy. Jessica Kingsley Publishers. London and Philadelphia (pp. 137, 138, 20, 29, 62, 63, 75, 72)
1. Grossburth, P. (1986). Melanie Klein: Her world and her work. New York: Alfred A. Knopf, Inc. www.webster.edu/˜woolfilm/klein.html#play
2. En.wikipedia.org/wiki/John Bowlby
3. Schroeter, V. (2002). Summary of Research on Mother Infant Bonding. The Clinical Journal of the International Institute for Bioenergetic Analysis,(12)
4. Siegel, D. Hartzell, M. (2003). Parenting From the Inside Out. Penguin Group. New York

Bioenergetic Analysis and Contemporary Psychotherapy: Further Considerations

Dialoging with Other Modalities and the Neurosciences[1]

Angela Klopstech

Summary

This article attempts to make a case for the integration of neuroscience research and theory into the field of Bioenergetic Analysis, and body psychotherapy in general. It is argued that such an integration might lead to a better dialogue between body psychotherapies and more traditional schools of therapy.

After discussing basic neuroscience terms a basic bioenergetic concept, "energetic charge", is reviewed in the light of neuropsychological models; in this context the concept of a "window of tolerance" comes into play.

Then, illuminated by the description of two concrete therapy situations, the author demonstrates how body oriented interventions might have an influence on brain activity. This, it is argued, points to the necessity of more focus on the body in traditional psychotherapy, as well as to the necessity of integrating appropriate body oriented interventions into the repertoire of traditional psychotherapy. In this context, a propositon for 'multi-lingual' understanding and language, bioenergetic, neuropsychological and relational, is made, in order to ease our communication with other modalities.

Keywords: neuroscience, limbic system, optimal arousal level, mirror neurons, body-oriented interventions

---

1 Keynote speech delivered at the biannual Conference of the International Institute for Bioenergetic Analysis in Seville, Spain, May 2007

I. INTRODUCTION

There is considerable buoyancy in the broader therapy world surrounding Bioenergetic Analysis and we can be sailing on this full sea. Exciting developments in modalities such as EMDR, trauma therapy, and positive psychology, and in the arenas of the neuroscience, emotion theories and infant research are creating waves. And at the same time, the familiar waters of psychoanalysis and Jungian analysis are undergoing dramatic changes that have not adequately been explored by us.

Some years ago, I wrote "it is obvious that Bioenergetic Analysis can neither remain solely within the limitations of its original energy concepts, nor can it afford to lose its roots and become lost in the recent relational and process oriented approaches. In part, its viability will require that it expands its conceptual framework and cast a curious eye on the research from contemporary neuroscience. A continual reevaluation of old and integration of new concepts is necessary for surviving and thriving" (Klopstech 2005a, p. 101). While I still maintain strongly that we not lose our own center and become an eclectic mishmash, it seems to me that we have emerged from our splendid isolation and are more fully attempting to enter the mainstream with its attendant opportunities and dangers. We are expanding our conceptual frame, we are reevaluating our key concepts, and, particularly, we are casting a curious eye toward infant research and the neurosciences. This paper will explore some of the exciting and challenging possibilities for linkage.[2]

First, an overview of some potential linkages with other therapeutic modalities at present will be provided. This will be brief and buzzword-like, so that developments or connections familiar to the reader may be detected, but mainly so that new buzzwords or better 'buzzconcepts' of interest may be discovered and followed up on. Two separate prisms will be used for this purpose: a.) just naming the therapeutic modality – e.g. psychoanalysis – and listing some dialoguing efforts by topic and authors, and b.) defining core issues and concepts that are being re-thought by us, as well as by other modalities.

Second, I will delve more deeply into an area that I am passionate about, and that is the impact of neuroscience research on Bioenergetic Analysis and the broader world of psychotherapy.

---

2 It is part of a series of papers and presentations in which I deal with the broader topic of exploring and defining the place of Bioenergetic Analysis in the contemporary psychotherapy world (Klopstech 2000a, 2000c, 2000d, 2004a, 2004b, 2005a, 2000b).

II. LINKAGES WITH OTHER THERAPEUTIC MODALITIES AT PRESENT

a.) Bioenergetic Analysis in Dialogue with Neighboring Psychotherapies

Bioenergetic Analysis and Psychoanalysis:
  Enlarging the Therapeutic Frame (Heisterkamp 1993; Geißler 1995, 2002; Hoffmann-Axthelm 1996; Klopstech 2000a, 2000c; Moser 2001; Koemeda 2002)

Bioenergetic Analysis and Contemporary Psychotherapy: Further Considerations
  Relationality, Intersubjectivity and Mutuality (Aaron and Anderson 1998; Heinrich 1999;
  Cornell, 2000, Lewis 2004, 2005)
  Relationality, Modes of Therapeutic Action (Stark 1999; Carle, L. 2000, Hilton, B. 2000; Klopstech 2000d)
  Gender and Sexuality revisited (Cornell in press; Klopstech 2004b; Hoffmann-Axthelm 2007)

Bioenergetic Analysis and Jungian Analysis:
  Jung and Reich (Conger 1988)
  Archtypes, mythical figures and their embodiment (Collier and Goodrich Dunn; Klopstech 2000b)

Bioenergetic Analysis and Trauma Therapies, EMDR
  (Berceli 1999; Eckberg 2000; Lewis 2000; Resneck-Sannes 2002; Maley 2006)

Bioenergetic Analysis and the broader world of Body Psychotherapy:
  (Analytical Body Psychotherapy, European Association for Body Psychotherapy, United States Association for Body Psychotherapy)

b.) Core Concepts which are Being Re-Thought by Other Modalities as well as by Us

➤ *passion, libido and sexuality* (Psychoanalysis),
➤ *contemporary models of self: multiple, evolving selves?* (neurosciences, infant research, some schools of psychoanalysis),
➤ *the multifactorial, frustratingly elusive definition of emotions* (emotion theories, neuroscience, positive psychology, EMDR)
➤ *human development between the poles of person/body in relation to itself and in relation to others* (theories of emotion, neuroscience, infant research, relational psychoanalysis)
➤ *autonomous and dyadic self regulation* (neuroscience, infant research, relational psychoanalysis)
➤ *unconscious-which unconscious?* (Psychoanalysis, neuroscience)
➤ *body-based theories of the mind and plasticity of the brain* (infant research, neuroscience)

III. INTEGRATING NEUROSCIENCE

In a relatively new interdisciplinary endeavor where "the best of modern science [converges] with the healing art of psychotherapy" (Siegel in Schore, 2003a, Preamble), data from neurobiology and neuropsychology are applied to understand and describe the origin and development of the self. What emerges from this convergence and meeting of the various fields of neuroscience, infant research and psychotherapy theories is a complex, dynamic and holistic (brain-mind-emotion-body) view of the human being and of human interaction, a view that is clinically applicable and, at times, experimentally testable. This new knowledge and scientifically based understanding is of particular importance for us as bioenergetic therapists because it relates to the interplay of body, mind, emotion and interpersonal relations, which is at the heart of our therapeutic enterprise. It is called interpersonal or affective neuroscience and emphasizes the basic role that brain bodily phenomena play in the process of change. At the same time, there is no coherent or good conceptualization of the place of the actual physical body, and it is here that neuroscience can meet Bioenergetic Analysis. My presentation is an attempt at some bridging between the neurosciences and Bioenergetic Analysis, This integration can allow us to rethink what we do bioenergetically in neuroscience terms; it can enable us to speak neuroscience language as a second language (or third if you think of relational language as our second language). And because this second language is fast becoming the common language for various schools of psychotherapy, we may actually begin to understand each other and talk to one another in a dialogue fashion, rather than in collective monologues. As a consequence, I argue, we as Bioenergetic therapists will become more eloquent in getting across to our therapy neighbors what we have to offer.

A number of cognitive therapies, trauma therapies and some psychoanalytic schools have done a better job than us in bridging their theories and understanding of therapeutic process to neuroscience. Particularly relational psychoanalysis, which I consider a close professional neighbor, has responded to neurobiological research and studies of mother/infant interaction with a rigorous rethinking of its understandings of human development and the psychoanalytic process. One outcome among others is a changed notion of the dynamics within the therapeutic dyad (Boston process of change group, Tronick et al. 1998, Schore 2003a, 2005). But relational psychoanalysis has failed to adequately update their conceptualization of the body and bodily phenomena, and there is again an absence of any nuanced conceptualization of the place of the body. It is here that Bioenergetic Analysis meets both Psychoanalysis and Neuroscience. Only recently, have we, as Bioenergetic therapists, begun to consider the implications of neuroscience to our field with a series of articles and speeches (e. g. Klopstech 2005a, 2000b, Koemeda 2004, Koemeda & Steinmann 2003, Lewis 2004, Resneck-Sannes 2003a, 2003b) and some private communication between the authors. I will be referring to their work later in my paper.

I believe that integrating neuroscience into Bioenergetics should be much more than paying lipservice by bowing in its direction. This area needs to be part of our curriculum and our everyday practice. Why would this be important? Verbal methods and symbolic processing have always been, and still are, the goldstandard for how to conduct therapy. It is at this crucial point that neuroscience provides a breakthrough for what matters in psychotherapy, and that is that VERBAL PROCESSES ALONE ARE NOT ENOUGH ANY MORE! This notion is gaining increasing momentum in the general psychotherapy arena, and neuroscience is establishing it as a fact, not an assumption, not a question. For the first time from outside of body psychotherapy, the body is treated as an active and necessary protagonist for understanding development and process in psychotherapy, rather than being considered helpful at best and not essential at worst. Because of neuroscience research, contemporary psychotherapy shows increasing interest in nonverbal interpersonal communication and in nonverbal processing, i. e. dealing with emotion, all of which is definitely our area of expertise. This presents for us an opportunity that we cannot forego, a chance we would be foolish to miss and a challenge that we need to meet.

Now, what do I actually mean when I say 'integrating'? Integrating means fully absorbing neuroscience research and models into Bioenergetic theory and practice *and* making good use of it in a way that dialogue becomes possible with neuroscience and the larger psychotherapy community. But real dialogue and 'crossfertilization' depends on both sides having something to offer. I think it is ironic that we have real goodies to offer, i. e. a profound understanding of the role of the body in human development and interaction, but nobody except us really knows this; partly because of our arcane language, partly because of our ideosyncratic albeit useful concepts, partly because of their adherence to an obsolete touch taboo, and partly because of their essentially limitating the body to the face and facial expression.

So, this paper wants to contribute to establishing a common language, with re-evaluating some of our basic concepts in the light of this language, and with demonstrating the value of body-to body-interaction for the broader psychotherapy world. Bob Lewis (2005) and Helen Resneck-Sannes (2005) gave presentations at the last convention in Brazil in a similar vein, and I hope they started a tradition which I am now continuing.

Let's look at:
1) *What neuroscience offers us:* A re-evaluation of our foundational concepts and a common language that makes us contemporary and able to link with mainstream psychotherapy.
2) *What we offer to the neurosciences and the broader psychotherapy world:* Bodily interventions can have an impact on re-organizing processes of the brain. It thus becomes sensible for these modalities to integrate appropriate body oriented interventions into their repertoire.

Before I can address these issues more fully, I will provide a Brief Overview of Relevant Neuroscience Terms, Data and Models (brief, because of spatial constraints and my neuroscience understanding that if it were too long I exponentially increase the probability of losing my readers. Also, this is meant to be a motivational paper, i.e. motivating readers to want to learn this language; not actually learning it here and now.)

Comprehensive summaries of neuroscience data and their application to psychotherapy (in the English speaking world) are provided in several voluminous books by Damasio (1994, 1999), Schore (1994, 2003a, 2003b) and Siegel (1999). Their writings are fascinating, complicated and here is my condensed and very, very simplified version.

Although the brain functions as an integrated whole, it is comprised of different systems. So, consider two ways of understanding brain structure and function, an lower-upper view and a right-left view: There is a lower area: the limbic system, the so called 'emotional brain' that is involved in the perception and regulation of emotions and bodily states. This is also the place where our early interaction experiences are stored. They are stored not as explicit, conscious knowledge, but as 'implicit knowledge', i.e. preconscious knowledge that is not verbal, but with the potential of becoming conscious and verbalized. And there is an upper area, on top of and surrounding the lower area limbic system. This is the neo-cortex, with its different parts, that are involved in reflection, reasoning, associating, planning etc.

Now that we have done the upper-lower, let's go left-right. The left hemisphere primarily communicates with the pre-frontal cortex and the right hemisphere primarily communicates with the limbic system. The right brain has been linked to the implicit, i.e.unconscious and preconscious processing of bodily information that is embedded in emotional conversation and interaction; it is also linked to such crucial nonverbal and verbal therapeutic agents as attention and empathy. As Bioenergetic Analysts, we are working a lot with the right hemisphere and the limbic system.

Schore (2003a, 2003b) has developed a concept of 'dual-hemisphere regulation', i.e. both right-brain and left-brain self regulation, that provides one possible, and for our purposes very useful, organizing frame. He distinguishes between two different forms of regulations, the conscious, voluntary and verbal control of emotional states of the left brain and a nonverbal regulation of the right-brain. The more conscious and explicit "top-down" process (from higher cortical areas to subcortical limbic areas) of mainly the left hemisphere (LeDoux 1996, p. 172) is familiar to us as the concept of 'self- control' or 'we change the way we feel by changing the way we think'. It is at the core of cognitive psychology and cognitive psychotherapy. Of more recent vintage is the research on the regulation function of the right brain which is is a "bottom-up" process, involving the reception and expression of emotions. This process is relevant for the nonverbal or preverbal, body-to-body communication between therapist and patient, which is the essence of our ways of working. Together both sides of the brain share in the task of processing information and regulating emotion, but with different functions and different patterns of cortical-limbic connections, top-down and left and bottom-up and right. Schore's regulation theory suggests that implicit mechanisms lie at the core of major change processes and that the right brain, (the limbic system and the orbito-frontal cortex), plays a dominant role in psychodynamically oriented psychotherapy. 'Implicit mechanisms' basically means, that therapist and pa-tient are involved in dealing with emotions and emotional memory that they are only partially aware of, often bringing them to consciousness via what is now frequently referred to as 'right-brain' and/or 'limbic' attunement.

Equally important, but easier to grasp is Schore's understanding of the in-teractional nature of self regulation. He distinguishes between an interactive, person-to-person and a non-interactive intraperson mode, and he emphasizes that good therapy and a well functioning therapy dyad involve flexible and sensible use of both modes.

Now that we have some frame for brain functioning and how it is concep-tualized in interpersonal neuropsychology, let's go back to

What Neuroscience Offers Us

What might the actual application and integration of neurobiological and neuropsychological findings into the therapeutic domain look like, and which kind of new language could be used? The concept I have chosen here for purposes of illustration is *energetic charge level*. It is basic to our work and for some controversial.

High charge, low charge: Historically, the therapeutic value of high arousal and intense feelings has been at the heart of our therapy model, initially unquestioned, then heatedly debated, at times thrown overboard, but ever-present even when avoided. There has always been a dichotomy between low charge/energy and high charge/energy work: when, how much, with whom and so on. This therapy issue has not only divided *us* at times, but also has kept us apart from the mainstream which tended and tends to frown upon the concepts of arousal/charge/excitement as legitimate elements of therapy. Their accompanying Cassandra-cry was overstimulation and re-traumatiza-tion and we responded to it with either defending or posturing (depending on our character), claiming to be able to touch our patients more 'deeply' i.e. profoundly. The good news: it turns out that both sides are right some of the time, so let's take a closer look.

Neuroscience findings and models (Greenberg 2002, Siegel 1999, Traue 1998, 2005, Hüther 2005, Schiepek 2003) show the value and even necessity for some arousal level for neural restructuring in the limbic brain to occur. When you look at the relevant literature, the magic words are 'optimal stress', 'neu-roendocrine stress reaction', 'high emotional arousal', 'window of tolerance'. And some scientists/practitioners are dealing with the implications of these findings for the therapy process, i.e. defining the specific conditions under which heightened arousal can have a therapeutic effect. I will be combining Greenberg's and Siegel's models to provide insight into the neurophysiological underpinnings of the clinical debate regarding charge level.

Greenberg believes that intensity, expression and reflection are major agents of change. With regard to therapeutic interventions, Greenberg reviews research that provides evidence for the close connection between emotional arousal, depth of experience, emotional focus and therapy outcome. What is relevant for us here is that Greenberg finds that " high emotional arousal plus high reflection on emotional experience distinguish good and poor outcome cases, but that arousal and expression of emotion *alone* may be inadequate in promoting change" (Greenberg, 2002, p. 13). On the basis of these findings he concludes that emotional arousal needs to be combined with meaning construction and reflection, i.e. with a process of metabolizing and integrating high intensity experiences for it to be clinically useful. This is what we used to call 'working through'.

The therapeutic model developed by Siegel does not deal with the 'qualita-tive' factor of arousal/intensity/charge, but rather with the 'quantitative' one. Siegel does not focus on arousal as a therapeutic agent per se, but he asks 'how much is too much/not enough/for whom and when'. Relating to the literature and data from neurobiology and trauma theory he defines a 'window of tolerance' as the optimal frame for arousal in order to process emotionally loaded material: "one's thinking or behavior can become disrupted if arousal moves beyond the boundaries of the window of tolerance" (Siegel, 1999, p. 254). The window of tolerance connotes a dynamic quality that involves the movement of affective or energetically charged material from limbic structures to the upper right and/or left brain so that expression can occur, either implicit, e.g. with a gesture or a vocal uttering, or conscious, linguistic and narrative. Windows of tolerance will differ among people. "For some persons this window may be quite narrow, for others a wide range of emotion may both be tolerable and available to consciousness. How open the individual window is for a specific person at a specific time depends on his/her inner circumstances and the social context, and it is different at different times" (Siegel, 1999, p. 254).

Siegel's concept emphasizes the individuality and variability of arousal levels with regard to their therapeutic usefulness. This becomes a guideline for therapeutic action: therapy only works well when it takes place within the window of tolerance, therapists only work well when they stimulate or calm down, attuning to this specific patient in this specific situational context. The interpersonal context, the dyadic regulation is of immense importance. Resneck-Sannes (2005, p. 38) refers to this as the 'therapeutic window' and describes in detail how bioenergetic therapists can actually work within this window.

Greenberg's and Siegel's positions have been at the center of our clinical practice and our theoretical discussions forever. We have had polarized debates about the merits of high charge versus low charge, mobilizing and soothing techniques, with defined camps of hardliners where only 'energizing blocks' and 'breaking through resistance' counted, or soft Bioenergetics where mobilizing and raising energy levels in itself was already considered bad therapy. The neuroscience that I have briefly summarized provides enough evidence for what most of us, I hope, intuitively have been paying attention to and actually practiced: how much charge is too much/not enough/for which patient and at which point in the therapy process; in summary: what does 'charge' mean for how one does relate to *this* patient in *this* context. Compared to therapists that rely on verbal and interactional explorations, our knowledge of bodyreading and character, and our expansive repertoire of indirect and direct body interventions gives us a huge advantage in the arena of regulation within the therapeutic window. We know both how to create low and high arousal and how to work with it, e. g. how to ground arousal. In this context "grounding a patient" means nothing more than bringing the patient into his/her window of tolerance.

What we have been missing so far is a language, that translates our concepts (in this instance, charge and grounding) and our ways of working into a language understood, accepted and used in the contemporary broader therapy world (arousal, window of tolerance). We have been hampered by the fact that 'energy' and 'charge' remained mushy concepts. For a variety of reasons beyond the scope of this paper, I do not propose abandoning these notions, but I believe it is necessary to integrate terms and concepts such as arousal, implicit/explicit knowledge, limbic system, regulation theory, dyadic regulation, window of tolerance and so on, into our bioenergetic language and tool kit.

Because of spatial constraints I have provided only this one example of integrating neuroscience thinking. In the example, I briefly touch on our concept of grounding, which deserves a fuller re-evaluation in neuroscience terms. This will be explored in a subsequent paper. Another good candidate for re-evaluation and integration of neuroscience ideas is our concept of catharsis; it is right in the the middle of a debate about the advantages and merits of high charge/low charge as agents of change. Cathartic experiences, if proccessed well, can be good examples for neurological restructuring: there is the high arousal (Greenberg), there is the combination of arousal with expression, meaning and reflection (again Greenberg), there is the emergence of changed emotional information from lower, limbic structures to upper brain structures (Schore), together with the right brain-left brain processing (Schore again) and there is the therapeutic window (Siegel).[3]

Let's turn now to an essential contribution which we can offer to both affective neuroscience and the broader therapy world. The contribution consists of the knowledge of

---

3 I have explored the concept of catharsis and its re-thinking in neuroscience terms in earlier publications (Klopstech 2004a, 2005a).

How Bodily Interventions May Influence the Re-Organization of the Brain

First, small segments from two therapy sessions will be presented and subsequently compared and contrasted using bioenergetic as well as neuroscience language and perspective. These segments are cursory and moment-focused. They have the character of snapshots, embedded in and enriched with some background information. I call them clinical moments. Bear with me, there is a reason why I present two clinical moments in a row.

Clinical Moment 1:
The following situation takes place after about half a year of weekly therapy. The patient is a young woman, Athena, in her early twenties, an art student, who grew up in Italy and in New York City, in a household suffused by art. Her father is French and her mother American, and the parents divorced when she was twelve years old. She entered therapy because, after having lived in Italy during her high school years, she wanted very much to live and work in New York, but felt increasingly 'confused' about this enterprise unable to concentrate on her work here or develop a circle of friends, and yearning back for Italy. Up to this point, we had generally worked with a mixture of talk and autonomous and interactive grounding techniques, starting with some verbal interaction in my office chairs and moving into some physical work from there. The story of her un- and uprooted life began to unfold for us and she realizes that it is about creating her own roots now, here in New York, in school, with her friends and with me.

This session is starting differently. My patient does not sit down in her chair immediately, as usual; she rather stops, standing next to it, tentatively, looking around. I walk over to her, look around with her and ask, also tentatively: "You are looking for something...?" Her gaze turns to the floor, and she says that she would rather like to sit there, which she then does. At the same moment, before she even utters her words, I "know" what she has in mind, a barrage of images from the last sessions is flooding my mind: I become aware how uncomfortable and stiff, like squeezed in, she appeared as soon as she sat down in her chair. I obviously noticed all this before, but it had not reached the threshold of consciousness to use actively in therapy. I feel a palpable sense of relief in mind and body about Athena's action/solution and I let her know.

She smiles, approvingly, as I sit down, half next to her and half across from her. Her body seems not only to let down on the office floor, but also seems to take up more space in my office, now that she is not confined to a chair. As she is talking, her legs extend as if by chance in my direction. I lean my body forward, her toes reach my feet and come to rest there.

For many of the following sessions we start with a similar position, both of us on the floor, her toes somehow up against my body. As we sit this way, she shares more and more about what is happening inside her when we are in this position. It makes her feel "at home" and her words flow with more ease. It is easier to be "with me" rather than across from me" which made her feel separate, though the actual distance between the upper parts of our bodies was approximately the same as when we were sitting on our chairs, face to face. Now, sitting on the floor, we have the bodily bridge of 'her-toes-to-my-body' to reduce distance and amplify connection. At times I just listen, responding with my body, leaning toward her or away, shifting with her, picking up the slightest change in her feet/toes movement to stay connected, letting my body be shaped according to hers. At other times I respond not only with my body, but also with words and we get engaged verbally. She reports that she is actively finding and creating her space, physically and emotionally, not only in my office but in her larger life in New York, creating friendships and becoming involved in art projects with other students. Memories emerge for her about sitting at the family dining table: how she had to stay in her place, her hands on the table not daring to change her position, not daring to speak up to her overbearing father. For a number of sessions the contact with our feet, somehow, remains important in the therapy. It also appears important that she can move her hands freely: "My hands belong totally to me, they are my tools" (she is an artist, painting, sculpting, sewing, soldering).

Clinical Moment 2:
The following cathartic situation occurs after three months of therapy. The patient is a forty year old woman, Sarah. She entered therapy with me because of a lifelong history of not liking her body, and because of recent marital strife. She had been in body psychotherapy before, so bodywork is familiar to her and the first three months of therapy consisted of a mix of verbal interaction with physical interventions. At this point in therapy, we are both aware that a big part of her life involves fighting, starting with her family of origin in

South America and continuing here in the US where she started out as an immigrant without a green card, rising to become a well regarded physician. Sarah's fighting mentality is manifested in a hard muscled body with the strong jaw of a warrior. Her overdeveloped calves and thighs insure that nobody will push her over!

She feels understood and accepted in the relationship with me, and so, three months into the therapy, I decide to offer her an intervention, deliberately not telling her beforehand my reasons for this specific choice of intervention so as not to influence her reaction, I tell her that I want to carry her on my hands and explain the technique: I will lie down on the floor, on my belly with my arms extended forward and my palms turned upward, resting on the ground. She will walk slowly onto my hands so that the soles of her feet will actually rest on my hands. My patient is okay with the notion of exploring her feelings and reactions in this setting without, to begin with, explicitly knowing why we are doing this admittedly strange enterprise together. We agree to talk afterwards about my underlying assumptions.

The basis for this intervention comes from my understanding of her history, i. e. there was a severe lack of parental support in her family life, paired with the simultaneous burden of having to care for younger siblings and having to make it in the world. Going back to the literal root of the word 'support', which means 'to carry from below', I offer the physical experience of 'supporting' her body and weight from below and hope that her body gets the message that support is something that exists and can be literally experienced.

Sarah's immediate reaction is surprise, disbelief and the concern that she will be too heavy, followed by an apprehensive, affirmative nod of her head. I can feel in my hands how she is letting down more and more, giving me more of her weight, relying on me to support her. She tells me how relieving this feels to her. Then I hear a deep sigh and she breaks into a strong sobbing that shakes her whole body … but she remains on my hands … crying for a long time. What comes to her mind when the sobbing abates is something she has not realized before: how much she criticizes and bosses her husband around with sentences like "Why didn't you do …?". She is horrified. I say to her "demands harden and wishes soften". She is quiet … I ask her to slowly leave my hands and to move back onto her feet. She experiences the ground as softer than before, with more give. I ask: "The way you would like to be?"

The next session Sarah tells me that during the past week she made a point of asking her husband rather than demanding and that she felt less exhausted than usual. "Also" she says half embarrassed, half fascinated "sex was much better".

Compare and contrast, using a multi-frame approach[4]

The two clinical moments are not atypical for clinical work in body psychotherapy and they share essential similarities. Of course we can look at them through our familiar lenses, psychodynamically, bioenergetically, relationally, but for our current purposes, they also lend themselves well to a neuropsychological understanding. I will switch back and forth between the different lenses to demonstrate how enriching multicentered language and understanding can be. My specific reference will be to the new language we are trying to grasp, neuropsychological language.

Both clinical moments can be viewed as corrective experiences that attempt to create new neurological connections involving right-brain-to-right-brain-then-left-brain sequences, both involve flexible self-regulation, i.e. autonomous, within-my-patient regulation and dyadic, between-her-and-me regulation. And in both situations my patients remained within their windows of tolerance, though the arousal levels were quite different, and shaped the course of the therapy differently. Our bioenergetic language would emphasize the essential role of physical contact for change, the specific interventions that I made, e.g. body-to-body, the role character assessment and body reading played and so forth. A relational view might for example focus on the specificity of the relationship, e.g. Sarah's and my interaction around her concerns of being "too much", or Athena's and my converging attemps to make my office a new good " home" for her, as transitional space for making New York a good home.

Now, more specifically, in both clinical moments the communication between my patients and myself take place using verbal language and also body language. It is a conversation with words and a conversation with gestures, literally with "hands and feet". This conversation can, on one hand,

---

4 Some reflections in this particular chapter are an updated and expanded version of a similar line of thinking in an earlier publication (Klopstech, 2005b, p. 100–103)

be understood as an attempt to "talk" to the patient's limbic system which does not understand verbal language but seems to understand the emotional content of language and the language of the body. But it can also be seen as a communication between two limbic systems via a body-to-body interaction: it is about "listening with my limbic system" via my body "It is the body of the therapist that is the primary instrument for psychobiological attunement" (Lewis 2003, p. 59) and it is about "talking to the patient's limbic system" also via my body. Both moments work with flexible self-regulation, i.e. a mix of autonomous regulation where the patient uses inner resources without help from the therapist, and interactive regulation, back and forth, between patient and therapist. The new experience does not necessarily have to become verbalized or even conscious -a new buzzword for this is 'right-brain-to-right-brain-then-left-brain sequence'- in order to have a regulating effect on thoughts, behavior, feelings. Instead, it may play itself out below the threshold of awareness -buzzword again- 'right-brain-to right-brain'.

In our bioenergetic language, energetic changes are complex entities made up of more or less conscious microelements, ranging from a subtle change in the quality of the eye contact or the quality of touch, to obvious changes in breathing patterns, emotional states and thought processes, and to changes in verbal expressions. Athena's body movements, her head nod, the extension of her feet, repeated in every session provide a good example for the complexity. The connection via our feet and legs, for example, was silently acknowledged but never a word was exchanged about the significance, a typical limbic or right-brain-to right-brain communication. And remember Sarah, emotionally experiencing, relishing the support of her body through my body, right-brain-to right-brain communication, and then her verbalized insight about being overcritical and bossy with her husband, i.e. now the upper left brain comes into play. As you could hear, I used what I call ' brain pinball language' to illustrate the translatability of neuroscience language into bioenergetic clinical event language.

With its direct bodily interventions and explorations Bioenergetic Analysis possesses an excellent, and expansive repertoire of techniques, which, when embedded in an appropriate relational field ('old' psychodynamic language: transference and countertransference) *can* become the carriers of both relationship and communication between limbic systems. How much repetition of essentially the same experience, interactional and intrapersonal, or how much variation within one experience pattern is necessary for the weakening or overwriting of an old neurological connection and the creation of a new one? We don't know and the answer is left to the belief system, assessment or intuition of the therapist. As an aside, I do not believe that all physical or physical relational work leads to neural restructuring. The subset that seems more likely to lead to reorganization of limbic structures consists of those interventions and explorations that trigger important, perhaps traumatic biographical material. If, in additon to the ontogenetic, i. e. biographical information, phylogenetic material in deeper subcortical areas is also touched upon, it may increase the chances of reorganization. This issue will be adressed in a subsequent paper.

The two clinical moments also differ in important ways. The first one deals with a spontaneous "enactment" between Athena and myself. I understand "enactment" as a co-created constellation, i. e. a "production" created jointly by therapist and patient, often in the non-verbal arena, where it is not clear-cut who reacts to whom, who instigated an action and whose actions are a mere consequence of the other's actions. The second one, on the other hand, is based on a hypothesis-guided action by me and results in a cathartic experience for my patient Sarah. My intervention is based on a conglomerate of different pieces of background information: verbal input from Sarah, both about her life history and current situation, my reading of her body, comparing notes with her about how she knows her body, and my assessment of the relational field, i. e. the momentary and underlying transference-countertransference situation.

Also, the arousal levels in the clinical moments are different. The first is not cathartic and the therapeutic agent seems to be a repetitive low charge dyadic regulation with small variations in each session, easily within Athena's window of tolerance. The arousal level is nevertheless high enough for Athena for change to take place, she becomes increasingly grounded in her actions in life, i. e. in reality. There is an 'energetic insight', but the insight is on my, the therapist's side.[5]

---

5 By 'energetic insight' I mean the cognitive insight that goes together with the actual physical and emotional experience of a shift inside. The crucial component here is the almost-simultaneity of thought/feeling/body sensation. The simultaneous emergence and togetherness makes for the depth of experience and the experience of a shift inside (Klopstech 2005d, p. 60).

My implicit knowledge of how uncomfortable Athena was in her chair all of a sudden crystallized into explicit knowledge, and became the trigger event for subsequent action i.e. seating myself with her on the floor. This specific moment, the change of positioning from chairs to the floor (but also the process as a whole) is an example of the way 'mirror neurons' function as a neural basis for empathy. The initial constellation, moving to the floor together, and moving my legs towards her toes suggests that my mirror neurons 'anticipate' my patient's movement intention.

The recent discovery of mirror neurons is helping neuroscientists to explain a backlog of enigmas. Mirror neurons are labelled this way, because they recreate the experience of others within ourselves, allowing us to put ourselves into the shoes of another person, and thus experience empathy. Mirror neurons are located in the premotor cortex, the area that plans movements, and they are connected to the limbic system, the brain's emotional region; thus, when my mirror neurons fire in reaction to my patient, it triggers empathic emotions -or limbic resonance- in me. If some physical movement is involved in the other, mirror neurons may be responsible not only for perceiving action, but also for understanding the movement, behavior intentions and emotions of the other. In a sense, we do not just see somebody's action, but also start to feel the actions as sensations in ourselves as if we are the actors. I believe that mirror neuron phenomena have wide applicability, and present a real breakthrough in the connection between neuroscience and the psychotherapy process.

The second situation, on the other hand, describes a cathartic experience for the patient, induced by my hypothesis-guided intervention. I consciously wanted to provide a bodily-emotional and potentially intense corrective experience. This did result in a high aroual situation of physical and interpersonal intensity, where the intensity or high arousal was mobilized by a specific physical technique with its specific meaning in a specific relational moment. It paved the way for catharsis and two insights and a new experience. One insight occurred right away in the therapy session (I am too bossy with my husband). The other occured outside of therapy, as a low charge integration process (her realization that sex was much better). The new experience was the better sex, possibly coming from a limbic restructuring, and her realization of this as an insight. This process was not characterized by repetition but rather by initial high arousal within Sarah's window of tolerance and an instantaneous change in meaning. This was followed by dyadic regulation and then integration into everyday life. In traditional Bioenergetic language this whole process would be called a breakdown (or removal of an energetic block) followed by a breakthrough.

IV. CONSEQUENCES FOR CLINICAL PRACTICE: CAN BODY-ORIENTED INTERVENTIONS AND EXPLORATIONS PLAY A ROLE FOR NEIGHBORING PSYCHOTHERAPIES?

I used the clinical presentations to illustrate both 'multilevel' understanding and ways of bringing therapy process into different languages: bioenergetic, psychodynamic, relational, neuropsychological. The committment and desire to do these forms of translations has implications for our relationship with neighboring schools. Mainly because of neuroscience they are becoming attentive to non-verbal communication involving the body (and not just the face). *They* are talking about it, are interested in it, but *we* do not speak their language. The cost to us is that we are not integrated into the broader world, the cost to them is that they don't have a wide array of tools and approaches that potentially can reach lower brain structures. But they are not body psychotherapists so what can they sensibly take from us and usefully metabolize? This is an important question and my current view is mainly based on the way I work, and some training that I provide to non-body oriented practitioners. For a preliminary and general answer we can draw some conclusions from the clinical moments and their discussion while a fuller elaboration requires a speech or an article in its own right.

I consider verbal-physical fields of meaning, and particularly body metaphors, like those experimented with in the clinical moments, as providing an essential contact boundary between Bioenergetic Analysis and our psychotherapy neighbours. Of course, an intervention like the patient standing on my hands to provide literal support and human grounding, will likely remain in the sole repertoire of Bioenergetic Analysis. But a change of the setting, spontaneous or deliberate, such as sitting on the floor or standing up, could be integrated into the clinical practice of verbal therapists, at least of those who want to include the body more in their practice and/or are experimenting with ways of reaching their patients subcortical structures. Then there are also the more familiar and socially accepted forms of touch, like 'taking-by the hand' or 'a hand-in the-back-or-on-the-shoulder', that could be differently explored. And finally, bodily interaction, *without direct physical contact*, may open up new doors. Again, taking body metaphors literally provides an easy way in. Think, for example, of a phrase like " I want my own space", a phrase therapists hear quite often. Literally exploring closeness, distance and positioning between patient and therapist, far and close, front-side-behind, in the full field of vision or from the corner of an eye, is a potential physical interaction without even breaking the touch taboo. An example of a different kind is the therapist simply adapting to the breathing rhythm of the patient, creating a physical attunement and a sense of togetherness, without body contact or explanatory words.

These examples can be understood and taught using traditional bioenergetic language and neuropsychological language aswell as relational language. If we become 'mulit-lingual', and if we can switch back and forth, or even be multicentered in our thinking and speaking, then we can *show* that we provide a necessary conceptualization of the the place of the actual physical body for neuroscience, and for non-body oriented therapy modalities.

V. FINAL REMARKS

So, you can see, that I am interested in and excited by what the broader therapy world is up to. But, after all, what has getting involved really done for me?

1) It has helped me maintain a vitality and freshness in my work, which is no small matter when there is therapy burnout around.

2) I can have a meaningful conversation with non-bioenergetic therapists, and at times I actually do.

3) I can't tell you that they are actually interested in what I do specifically. That has not happened yet, and believe me, I have tried. But I am sure this will change with therapists' growing interest in the body and the body's role in the therapeutic encounter, an interest essentially sparked by neuroscience.

4) I am now at the point where I myself am multi-centered when I work with patients. Both the Bioenergetic frame and the frames I have spoken about, neuroscience and relational, are in my conscious (explicit) mind and, from the way things pop up for me, they seem to be in my preconscious (implicit) mind also. I maintain that having this multiplicity of frames has made me a more effective therapist.

References

Aaron, L. und Anderson, F. S. (1998): Relational Perspectives on the Body, (The Analytic Press), Hillsdale NJ.

Berceli, D. (1999): Trauma and startle reflex: It's creation and resolution. Bioenergetic Analysis, vol 10, Nr 1, p. 11–15

Bauer, J. (2006): Warum ich fühle was du fühlst. (Hoffmann und Campe), Hamburg.

Carle, L. (2002): Das Beziehungsgeschehen in der Psychotherpie. Koemeda-Lutz, M. (2002) (ed): Körperpsychotherapie – Bioenergetische Konzepte im Wandel. (Schwabe), Basel. p. 88–116

Collier, E. and Goodrich-Dunn, B. (2002–2007): personal communications

Conger, J.(1988): The Body as Shadow. (North Atlantic Books), Berkeley.

Cornell, B. (2000): Tranference, desire and vulnerability in body centered psychotherapy. In: Energy & Character 20 (2), p. 50–60.

Cornell, B. (in press): The Impassioned Body: Erotic Vitality and Disturbance. The British Gestalt Journal.

Damasio, A. R. (1994): Descartes' error. (Grosset/Putnam), New York.

Damasio, A. R. (1999): The Feeling of What Happens. (Harcourt, Brace and Company), New York

Eckberg, M. (2000): Victims of Cruelty. (North Atlantic Books), Berkeley.

Geißler, P. (1995): Psychoanalyse und Bioenergetische Analyse: Im Spannungsfeld zwischen Abgrenzung und Integration. (Peter Lang), Frankfurt a. M.

Geißler, P. (2002): Psychoanalyse und Körper: Überlegungen zum gegenwärtigen Stand analytischer Körperpsychotherapie. In: Psychoanalyse und Körper, Nr. 1, Jg. 1, (Psychosozial-Verlag), Gießen. p. 37–81

Greenberg, L. S. (2002): Integrating an Emotion-Focused Approach to Treatment into Psychotherapy Integration. In: Journal of Psychotherapy Integration, Vol. 12, No 2, S.154–189.

Heinrich, V. (1999): Physical Phenomena of Countertranference: Therapists as Resonance Body. Bioenergetic Analysis, The Clinical Journal of the IIBA, vol 10, Nr 2, p. 33–54.

Heisterkamp, G. (1993): Heilsame Berührungen. (Pfeiffer), München

Heisterkamp, G. (2003): Basales Verstehen. Handlungsdialoge in Psychotherapie und Psychoanalyse. (Pfeiffer bei Klett-Cotta), Stuttgart.

Hilton, R. (2000): Bioenergetics and modes of therapeutic action. Presented at the International conference on Bioenergetic Analysis, Montebello, Canada, May 2000,

Hoffmann-Axthelm, D. (1996): Am anderen Ufer des Sprachflusses. Über den möglichen Umgang mit sprachlosem Entsetzen in der körperorientierten Psychotherapie. In: Hoffmann-Axthelm, D. (eds), Mit Leib und Seele. Wege der Körperpsychotherapie. Körper und Seele 4, (Schwabe), Basel, p. 213–240

Hoffmann-Axthelm, D. (2007): Die Kunst des Liebens. Sexualität und Sexualisierung im Spiegel des körperpsychotherapeutisch orientierten Handlungsdialoges. In: Geißler, P. and Heisterkamp, G. (eds), Psychoanalyse der Lebensbewegungen: Zum körperlichen Geschehen in der psychoanalytischen Therapie – Ein Lehrbuch. (Springer), WienNew York, p. 441–458

Hüther, H.(2005): Mein Körper-das bin doch ich... Neurobiologische Argumente für den Einsatz Körperorientierter Verfahren in der Psychotherapie. Psychoanalyse & Körper, 4.Jg. (2005), Heft 11, Nr.7, (Psychosozial-Verlag), Giessen. p. 7–24

Klopstech, A. (2000a): Alter Wein in neuen Schläuchen: Die Integration ursprünglicher und gegenwärtiger Konzepte in der Bioenergetischen Analyse. Unveröffentlichter Vortrag zum Kongress der Schweizerischen Gesellschaft für Körperpsychotherapie. Basel.

Klopstech, A. (2000b): Frauen-Rituale. Die vielen Facetten einer Frau, CD. (Bauer Verlag), Freiburg

Klopstech, A. (2000c): Psychoanalysis and Body Psychotherapies in Dialogue, Bioenergetic Analysis, Vol 11, Nr.1, p. 43–54.

Klopstech, A. (2000 d): The Bioenergetic Use of a Psychoanalytic Conception of Cure, Bioenergetic Analysis, Vol 11, Nr.1, p. 55–66.

Klopstech, A. (2004a): Im Kontext autonomer und interaktiver Selbstregulation: Katharsis im neuen Kleid. In: Geissler, P. (2004): Was ist Selbstregulation? Eine Standortbestimmung. (Psychosozial-Verlag), Giessen.

Klopstech, A. (2004b): Entering the Dyadic world of Transference and Countertranference: Done Well, a Daring and Delicate Endeavor, Paper presented to the Western Pennsylvania Forum for Relational and Body Psychotherapy

Klopstech, A. (2005a): Catharsis and Self-Regulation Revisited: Scientific and Clinical Considerations. In: Bioenergetic Analysis, The Clinical Journal of the IIBA, Vol. 15, No 1, p. 101–132

Klopstech, A. (2005b): Stellen die Neurowissenschaften die Psychotherapie vom Kopf auf die Füsse? Neurowissenschaftliche Überlegungen zu klassischen Konzepten der (Körper) Psychotherapie. Psychoanalyse & Körper, 4.Jg. (2005), Heft 11, Nr.7, (Psychosozial Verlag), Giessen. p. 69–108

Koemeda-Lutz, M. (2002) (ed): Körperpsychotherapie – Bioenergetische Konzepte im Wandel. (Schwabe), Basel.

Koemeda, M. (2004): Die relative Bedeutung von Kognition, Affekt und Motorik im psychotherapeutischen Prozess – eine bioenergetische Perspektive. Überarbeitete Version eines Vortrags beim Wiener Symposium „Psychoanalyse und Körper", September 2004. In: Geissler, P. (im Druck): Therapeutische Interaktion – Makro- und Mikroperspektive. (Psychosozial-Verlag), Giessen.

Koemeda-Lutz, M. & Steinmann, H. (2004): Implikationen neurobiologischer Forschungsergebnisse für die Körperpsychotherapie unter spezieller Berücksichtigung der Affekte. In: Koemeda, M. (ed) (2004): Neurowissenschaften und Psychotherapie. Psychotherapie Forum (12) No.2. (Springer), New York/Wien. P 88–97.

LeDoux, J. (1996): The Emotional Brain. (Simon & Schuster), New York

Lewis, B. (2000): Trauma and the Body. Bioenergetic Analysis, The Clinical Journal of the IIBA, Vol 11, No21, p. 61–76.

Lewis, B. (2004): Projective Identification Revisited: Listening with the Limbic System, Bioenergetic Analysis, The Clinical Journal of the IIBA, Vol 14, No 1, p. 57–74.

Lewis, B. (2005): The Anatomy of Empathy. Bioenergetic Analysis, The Clinical Journal of the IIBA, Vol 15, p. 9–31

Maley, M. (2006):Shock, Trauma and Polarization: Finding Unity in a world of Polarities. Bioenergetic Analysis, The Clinical Journal of the IIBA, Vol 1, p. 49–62

Moser, T. (2001): Berührung auf der Couch. Formen der analytischen Körperpsychotherapie. (Suhrkamp), Frankfurt a. M.

Resneck-Sannes, H. (2002): Psychobiology of affects: Implications for a somatic psychotherapy. Bioenergetic Analysis, The Clinical Journal of the IIBA, Vol. 15, No1, S.111–122

Resneck-Sannes, H. (2005): Bioenergetics: Past Present And Future, Bioenergetic Analysis, The Clinical Journal of the IIBA, Vol 15, No 1, p. 33–54.

Schiepek, G. (2003): Neurobiologie der Psychotherapie. (Schattauer), Stuttgart.

Schore, A. (1994): Affect Regulation and the Origin of the Self: The Neurobiology of Emotional Development. (Erlbaum), Hillsdale NJ.

Schore, A. (2003): Affect Regulation and the Repair of the Self. (Norton), New York.

Schore, A. (2003b): Affect Dysregulation and Disorders of the Self. (Norton), New York.

Schore, A. (2005): A Neuropsychoanalytic Viewpoint, Psychoanalytic Dialogues, 15, p. 829–854

Siegel, D. (1999): The Developing Mind. (Guidford Press) New York.

Siegel, D. (2003): Präambel. In: Schore, A. (2003a): Affect Regulation and the Repair of the Self. (Norton), New York.

Stark, M. (1999): Modes of Therapeutic Action. (Jason Aronson), Northvale, NJ.

Traue, H. (1998): Emotion und Gesundheit. (Spektrum), Heidelberg

Traue, H. (2005): Emotional Inhibition and Disease. Bioenergetic Analysis, The Clinical Journal of the IIBA, Vol. 15, No 1, p. 55–88

Tronick, E. Z., Bruschweiler-Stern, N., Harrison, A.M., Lyons-Ruth, K., Morgan, A.C., Nahum, J.P., Sander, L.W., Stern D.N. (1998): Non-Interpretative Mechanisms in Psychoanalytic Therapy. Int. J. Psycho-Analysis. 79, S. 903–921.

About the Author

Angela Klopstech has been a faculty member of the International Institute for Bioenergetic Analysis for more than 25 years, and has taught in training groups in both the US and Europe. She has major interests in the artful conceptualization of the therapy process, the role and importance of precise and evocative language, and the translation and bridging between the various domains of the psychological and the physical. She is currently in private practice in New York City.

Dipl.-Psych. Dr. Angela Klopstech
40–50 East Tenth Street, #1c
New York, NY10003
Tel/Fax: 212–2603289
klopkoltuv@aol.com

www.ingramcontent.com/pod-product-compliance
Lightning Source LLC
Chambersburg PA
CBHW020707270326
41928CB00005B/316